P9-APW-930

Salary Equity

Salary Equity

Detecting Sex Bias in Salaries among College and University Professors

Edited by
Thomas R. Pezzullo
Barbara E. Brittingham
University of Rhode Island

Lexington Books
D.C. Heath and Company
Lexington, Massachusetts
Toronto

52814

Library of Congress Cataloging in Publication Data

Main entry under title:

Salary equity.

Includes index.
1. College teachers—United States—Salaries, pensions, etc. 2. Equal pay
for equal work. I. Pezzullo, Thomas R. II. Brittingham, Barbara E.
LB2334.S23   331.2'81'378120973   78-24634
ISBN 0-669-02770-7

Copyright © 1979 by D.C. Heath and Company

All rights reserved. No part of this publication may be reproduced or transmitted in any form or by any means, electronic or mechanical, including photocopy, recording, or any information storage or retrieval system, without permission in writing from the publisher.

Published simultaneously in Canada

Printed in the United States of America

International Standard Book Number: 0-669-02770-7

Library of Congress Catalog Card Number: 78-24634

To David, Dan, and Grandma Stuebe

Contents

52814

Preface

The Civil Rights Act, the equal employment opportunity regulations and legislation, affirmative action programs, and philosophical and moral considerations of equity require that we pay close attention not only to employment opportunities but also to equal and fair treatment under such employment without regard to race or sex. The recent extension of the Equal Pay Act to college and university professors has heightened the interest of all postsecondary institutions in the nation on this very question. Widely accepted procedures for such analyses are yet to be developed. It is the purpose of this book to explore in depth one particular method, highlighting both its strengths and weaknesses, and to identify potential pitfalls for postsecondary institutions, advocacy groups, attorneys, economists, or equity agents.

The text is divided into three parts. Part I presents general information on the use of multiple linear regression in modeling faculty salaries. Glen Ramsay presents in technical terms a generalized multiple linear regression approach of particular interest to those contemplating conducting such an analysis. P. Kenneth Morse demonstrates the power of multiple regression by constructing misleading but plausible data. Those unfamiliar with multiple regression will find the analysis impressive. One of the remaining two chapters in this section is an introduction by the coeditors; the other is an analysis of the largest sample of faculty, their salaries, and related professional characteristics available. In this chapter Barbara Tuckman examines the effects of publication rates and types on salary rewards, as well as disciplinary differences in salaries.

Part II consists of five case studies in representative institutions around the nation. Each uses multiple linear regression, but in slightly different settings, with different institutional characteristics, and based on slightly differing assumptions and philosophy.

Part III consists of two dissenting views on the strict application of multiple linear regression to salary equity analysis. One takes the view that it is an appropriate technique but typically inappropriately applied; the other takes the view that statistical analyses alone cannot get at the idiosyncratic determiners of higher education salaries that are significant and not always unfair.

The production of this manuscript was by no means easy, especially in light of our desire to produce it in a timely way. Among the many people we must thank for helping with the background research and the manuscript preparation are Velna Murphy, Judy Haughton, Doug Rosie, Andrea Panciera, and Sylvia Feldman.

Thomas R. Pezzullo
Barbara E. Brittingham

Note: The use of the word *chairman* throughout this work denotes the person in charge of a department and applies to either gender. We consider the use of *chairperson* cumbersome and ineffective. We have tried to use *he* and/or *she* in combination to emphasize that *faculty member, dean, chairman, author, researchers*, and so forth, may be either gender.

**Part I
Using Multiple
Regression to Detect
and Estimate Sex Bias
in Salaries**

1

The Assessment of Salary Equity: A Methodology, Alternatives, and a Dilemma

Thomas R. Pezzullo and
Barbara E. Brittingham

This chapter describes the historical background leading to the recently height-ened interest in salary equity analyses and correction procedures. After a review of the many pitfalls that can be encountered by an institution desiring to conduct such a review and corrective action, the chapter concludes that the multiple linear regression, in one of its several forms, is the most reasonable and objective model for predicting salary and identifying potential inequities. The chapter also reviews the relevant literature on the subject and presents a frame of reference for the remaining chapters.

Nationwide, institutions of higher learning are scrambling to correct salary inequity, principally between men and women. Like all activities conducted under scrambling circumstances, the results are predictably uneven, helter-skelter, and very likely self-defeating. Institutions of postsecondary education have the most complex task of all employers: determining equitable salary for individuals with the same title but vastly different expertise, expectations, and salaries. American postsecondary institutions generally have the resources to do the more careful analysis required. General Electric can solve its technological problems and Chase Manhattan its financial problems, because they have the experts. Colleges and universities lay claim to some expertise in management and administration, economic and actuarial analyses, so each institution ought to be able to examine its salary patterns to determine whether, consciously or unconsciously, these patterns are inequitable.

They are compelled to do so by more than high motives. Executive Order No. 11246 and the Equal Pay Act of 1963 (later extended to include postsecondary education faculty) clearly mandate that men and women be paid equally for equal work. *Equal pay* is an easy determination; *equal work* determination is the source of the dilemma.

Methodology

The first likely pitfall in determining salary inequity is in selecting methodology. Several competing methodologies exist, each with its particular strengths and unfortunate weaknesses. To further complicate matters, applying more than one methodology to the problem yields vastly different results. It is therefore a matter of philosophy and general orientation to matters of compensation that dictates the choice of methodology and consequently determines the assessment of equity. The two most popular methodologies are the paired-comparison method and the actuarial method.

The Paired-Comparison Method

Many advocacy groups take the paired-comparison approach in order to demonstrate that inequity exists. Unfortunately, this method can be used only to demonstrate that inequity exists, not to determine its extent. It is limited to individual cases or to the comparisons made. Groups who choose the paired-comparison technique usually do so by choosing the most extreme cases—for the obvious motive of convincing the administration or trustees that salary inequities exist between men and women. To do that, one need only produce the most glaring examples of a man and a woman who appear equally qualified in terms of age, experience, highest degree, departmental affiliation, rank, and so forth. This procedure fails to assess the extent of inequity because it does not make every comparison possible. For example, both the man and the woman may have half a dozen colleagues more closely comparable on each of the salient variables—age, experience, highest degree, rank discipline, and so forth. The paired-comparison method is only a good first step.

The Actuarial Method

The actuarial method is a statistical extension of the paired comparison. In a simplified sense, it makes every conceivable paired comparison possible and looks at the "average" discrepancy. The specific statistical technique involved is known as multiple regression, a technique that examines correlational measures on a set of variables called *predictors* which are presumed (or known) to have a direct relationship with the *criterion*, that is, the variable to be predicted. College admissions offices use a number of variables to predict success in college by looking at a composite of age, aptitude test scores, rank in high school class, and grade point average in high school. By this process, the admissions office predicts success (the criterion) using multiple predictors. Later, of course, the prediction can be compared with actual performance.

One can similarly predict salary. An advantage in predicting salary instead of success in college is that actual salary is immediately available. The strength of the prediction of salary when examining any single predictor is in a sense a measure of the "effect" of that variable on salary. By looking at what one presumes to be the unbiased predictors of salary—rank, experience, highest degree, discipline, rank, years in the profession, scholarly activity—one can determine the maximum amount of salary variance that can be explained by biased predictors such as sex, race, political party membership, religious affiliation. For our purpose the only useful biased predictor in an equity analysis is sex. If the sex of the employee is entered into the regression analysis after the unbiased predictors have had their effect, the strength of its prediction can be a direct measure of inequitable consideration of salary. There is one major confounding effect, however. If an institution has knowingly or otherwise engaged in inequitable salary practices with regard to men and women, it may likewise have engaged in inequitable practices with regard to hiring, promotion, and certain circumstances conducive to scholarly and pedagogical achievements. If men and women have not had equal opportunity to earn advancement in the perquisites of higher-education faculty membership, then rank, discipline, and even qualitative variables may not be totally unbiased. However, if proper steps are taken in the first stages of a salary equity, the biasedness of these variables can itself be estimated.

A second confounding factor is the relationship between academic discipline and sex. To perform such an analysis in a comprehensive university requires that one first determine the extent to which women are overrepresented in certain traditionally female disciplines such as nursing, home economics, library science, and certain other service, home, community and health science assisting professions. If such overrepresentation exists, the determination of the disciplinary contribution to predicting salary may include some hidden sex bias. Translated into the plainest terms, this means that low nursing faculty salaries may be the consequence of that discipline's being low paid in general, which itself may be a consequence of the fact that that discipline is dominated by women. The extent to which it is one or the other is difficult to determine at the institutional level and impossible to determine nationally. Market factors and simple economics also have an impact on the average salary paid to a particular discipline. These market factors can be legitimate and may be related to supply and are more likely related to the interplay of supply and demand. The simple Marxian economic principle that supply should be the sole determiner of value just does not work in academia. If it did, the president of the university would be the lowest-paid employee, since whenever a vacancy occurs there, four to five hundred applicants make themselves available—a clear situation of oversupply. Conversely, certain low-paying positions tend to have a very small number of applicants.

History of Legislation

In recent years the movement to abolish sex discrimination in employment practices and to establish equity in pay has been supported by several major laws and regulations, both federal and state.

The first of these is the Equal Pay Act of 1963, which was adopted by Congress as a four-sentence amendment to the minimum wage provisions of the Fair Labor Standards Act of 1938 and originally designed to apply to sex discrimination in simple, routine jobs where performance differences were not significant in determining pay.

Other laws and regulations include specific references to employment practices in academe. Title VII of the Civil Rights Act of 1964 as amended by the Equal Employment Opportunity Act of 1972 prohibits discrimination in academic employment. Executive Order 11246 (as amended by 11375), issued in 1972 by the Department of Health, Education, and Welfare as part of its higher education guidelines, prohibits employment discrimination (including hiring, salaries, and upgrading) on the basis of sex and certain other factors; it also requires an affirmative action plan of all federal contractors.

In 1972 another significant piece of legislation affecting the regulation of employment and salary practices was enacted. The Education Amendments of 1972 changed the concept of the Equal Pay Act of 1963 by expanding coverage of the act to include executive, managerial, and professional workers, the category in which college and university faculty belong.

According to Lester (1975) that extension has caused perplexing and disturbing problems, especially for higher education faculty. The assumption inherent in the 1963 act, says Lester, is that workers should be paid according to job requirements and job conditions; that is, one should compare the jobs and not the individuals in the jobs in possible cases of illegal sex discrimination. However, in college and university settings

> professors are not customarily paid according to job content. From a general viewpoint, all professors perform roughly the same functions. Whether assistant, associate or full professors, they all engage in teaching and research and contribute in various other ways to intellectual life and effective operation of their departments and institutions.... The academic profession generally considers fair salary treatment to mean paying professors according to their contributions. Salary differentials are considered an indication of relative academic standing as well as a reward for accomplishments (Lester, 1975, p. 39).

The corresponding lack of guidelines from the Wage and Hour Division of the Department of Labor (charged with enforcing the act) has added to the difficulty of determining assumptions, approaches, and methods to be followed to enforce the act's provisions on the college or university level.

Other Inequity Studies

Several studies exploring the question of inequity and inequality in salaries in academe have been undertaken, some on an individual institution or small-group basis, and some nationwide. Inherent in all of them is the assumption that some form of discrimination in pay against women may exist; whether the studies can establish its existence with accuracy is another matter.

Recent descriptive data on the salaries of men and women faculty at the college and university level imply some discrimination and lay the groundwork for investigation. According to data released by the National Center for Education Statistics, gathered from full-time instructional faculty on nine-month or ten-month appointments, faculty salaries increased during the 1975-76 academic year by 6.1 percent. However, the average gain for men was 6.3 percent, while for women it was 5.8 percent. Average increases for men were larger than for women for all ladder ranks except full professor. Women constituted only 24 percent of the total number of faculty members reported in the survey—the same proportion as the previous year. However, additional data indicate that the proportion of women in full and associate professor positions decreased slightly from 1974 to 1975. Among universities included in the survey, the average difference between men's and women's salaries increased with rank.

Methods Used

We have already outlined some of the principal strengths of using multiple regression. According to Kieft (1974), its attractiveness lies in its flexibility; it can be adapted to any employee group at an institution without substantial modification of the methodology. Stepwise multiple regression is the method used by the American Association of University Professors (AAUP) in its salary and compensation studies; it is also the method utilized by Bayer and Astin (1975) in their replication study based on data from a nationally representative sample surveyed by the American Council on Education (ACE) in 1973.

The statistical approach also has its limitations. Several cautionary statements regarding the interpretation of the results have been made by both opponents and proponents of the method. For example, prediction equations are not without error; R^2 values of from 0.22 to 0.95 are reported in the literature. Also the data used tend to be retrospective, because "whatever discrimination there may be that prevents the employment of women as faculty is not observed [and since such studies] utilize the observed value of the predictor variables, such as discrimination in graduate school, that make it more difficult for women to obtain the doctorate, these effects are not taken into account" (Darland et al., 1973, pp. 129-130). Not taking into account the effects of any prior discrimination means that such analyses will tend to underestimate the degree of current inequity in salary.

Statistical studies attempt to predict salaries completely from a finite set of input variables even though most hiring and promotion policies place at least some, if not considerable, emphasis on hard-to-quantify attributes of the person being hired or promoted. In addition, a number of important attributes of a faculty member's performance can be entered into a statistical analysis only through tedious additional data collection which can be prohibitive in terms of both cost and time.

Results of Other Salary Studies

Common to all studies reviewed was the finding that women on the average receive lower salaries than men. Dorfman, in his 1975 AAUP survey on the status of the profession, reported that the average woman's compensation reported by all institutions with ranks was 17.5 percent lower than the average man's. According to Bayer and Astin (1975), in 1972-73 the average salary of academic men exceeded women's by more than $3,000.

The studies investigate the extent to which these differences can be attributed to relatively objective variables, such as rank, highest degree, productivity, and years of professional experience, and the extent to which they appear to be the result of discrimination in salary-setting procedures.

Bayer and Astin (1975) say that 22 percent of the variance can be explained by their predictor variables; the five most significant for both sexes appear to be (1) productivity as measured by articles published, (2) age, (3) degree level, (4) years of continuous service at present institution, and (5) time spent in administration. Darland et al. (1973), working with a set of more than twenty-five predictor variables, agree that when men and women are considered together, degree level, number of articles published, and the interaction term date of birth by number of articles are important for both sexes.

However, both Bayer and Astin and Darland et al. emphasize that although the predictors are important in determining salary, they are not always the same for men and for women; and when salary base and rank are controlled, Bayer and Astin find substantial differences between the two sets of predictor variables.

When salaries are predicted for men and women, the following results emerge. In almost every category, predicted salary for men is larger than that for women; whenever the predicted salary for men is large, the salary differential between men and women tends to be large; and it is in the senior ranks where the disparity is most pronounced.

The last finding deserves special attention because it is reported in almost all the literature reviewed. Bayer and Astin say that in the junior ranks (instructor, lecturer, assistant professor), remuneration for women about equals that for men; but at the senior, higher-paying levels, women had lower salaries than their male counterparts. Dorfman's AAUP report (1975) finds that the disparity in compensation is largest at the full professor rank; the average compensation for women professors is 8.4 percent lower. Darland et al. indicate that the increase in salary from age forty to age fifty is much less for women than for men almost without exception and that in general the differential that exists between men and women at all age levels is more pronounced for older women.

Bayer and Astin's explanation of this phenomenon is twofold: (1) the sex differential is largest for women who have been in the system longest and achieved high rank when sex discrimination was presumably greater, and (2) women of junior rank represent a pool of relatively new recruits and are rewarded on a par with male colleagues of comparable credentials.

Other findings suggested by these authors include the following.

1. The sex differential is due in part to differences in rates of promotion in rank.
2. No statistically significant sex differences exist among and within rank with respect to tenure.
3. The increase in salary with the period employed in academe is twice as much for men as for women.
4. Both gain by changing institutions, but men gain twice as much as women.
5. Men also gain twice as much by administrative activity.
6. Men who teach less are paid more, but women's salaries are unaffected by hours of teaching.
7. Men lose more than women by being employed part-time.
8. The underpayment of women is greater in research universities and in the physical and biological sciences.
9. In general, percentage differentials tend to grow as scholarly demands increase.

The conclusion drawn from these findings is virtually the same across the studies reviewed. As Dorfman puts it, there is "strong presumptive evidence that women are in weaker bargaining positions than men in the academic market place and are forced to accept inferior bargains" (1975, p. 123). Or, as Bayer and Astin say, "With the stress on the accrual of large numbers of publications, etc., the present reward system is more consistent with present professional roles and opportunities of male faculty members than of female" (1975, p. 801). Or as Darland et al. declare simply, "We must conclude that there is sex discrimination in faculty salaries" (1973, p. 129).

What possible factors lie behind these findings? Not all the authors are willing to speculate, but there is general agreement that unobserved variables account for a significant amount of the variance in salaries between males and females in academe. Several of these variables surface in a discussion of the merit system of reward, such as is generally found in colleges and universities.

Under such a system, increases in pay and rank are usually based on three factors: quality of teaching, quality of scholarship, and quality of service to the university community (Lester, 1975). A merit system can therefore open up the possibility that no two professors in the same department receive or deserve the same salary. Lester cautions that with all the individuality and subtlety in university salary structures under such a system, it is difficult to determine the extent of individual salary discrimination, if any, at a given institution. One must bear in mind that salaries are relative and linked in a network of relationships.

For example, quality of scholarship—research leading to publication—weighed heavily as a factor in determining salary in all the studies reviewed. Conflicting evidence has been reported about whether women publish as much or less than men. Centra, in his survey of 3,658 men and women who received doctorates in the years 1950, 1960, or 1968 (1974), reports that men publish more. Abramson (1975) cites two studies that say women are as productive. Bayer and Astin (1975) believe that the reward system is geared to the professional roles and opportunities males are more likely to enjoy; that is, they are simply more likely to be in a position requiring and conducive to scholarly production.

Several explanations for the reward system's tendency to favor men are offered by Abramson and Centra. Women, according to Abramson, are more likely to be found in positions in which research and publication are more difficult to produce. She cites 1973 Department of Labor statistics showing that women are more often found in small colleges and that those in larger universities are generally found in the lower ranks; in both situations the job emphasis is on teaching. Centra agrees, adding other influencing factors: women have less time for scholarship because of domestic responsibilities, and married women have less economic pressure to publish in order to increase income to support a family. It is interesting that publication rates for single men and single women tend to be similar.

Market factors also come into play in a merit system of reward: intercampus competition for faculty, the higher salary levels of certain disciplines, and the increase in demand for female faculty (mainly as a result of affirmative action pressure), which has tended to increase women's salaries (Lester, 1975).

Some market factors put women at an automatic disadvantage, with a resultant loss in bargaining power for salaries and promotion. As suggested by *Opportunities for Women in Higher Education*, a 1973 Carnegie Commission report, married women have less mobility and cannot easily take a better job at another institution, and they cannot convincingly use job offers to negotiate a promotion at their present institution. As for variations in salary by discipline, women are usually massed in departments with low salaries and are virtually absent from such high-paying disciplines as engineering. Married women also have frequently been considered secondary earners and thus less in need of salary or promotional increases (Abramson, 1975). Abramson criticizes this notion, arguing that no one has shown that financial need should govern salary decisions for men.

Darland et al. (1973) question whether salary differentials may be due in part to women's tendency to withdraw from the labor market during childbearing years, thereby decreasing their years of professional experience, another significant variable in determining salary. They state that highly educated women do not withdraw from the labor forces more than men, a claim supported by an American Council on Education survey (1973), which found that nearly a fourth of all faculty had interrupted their professional careers for more than one year and that a greater percentage of men than women did so.

All these comments underscore the role of unobserved variables in the determination of salary. They also demonstrate that the most exacting analysis of salaries cannot take into account the prior discrimination that leaves women at a disadvantage in what appear to be nondiscrimination variables (degrees, experience, publications) and other hidden conditions that differentially affect women in salary determination.

References

Abramson, Joan. *The Invisible Woman.* Washington, D.C.: Jossey-Bass Publishers, 1975.

Bayer, Alan E. "Teaching Faculty in Academe: 1972-73." Washington, D.C.: American Council on Education, 1973.

Bayer, Alan E., and Astin, Helen S. "Sex Differentials in the Academic Reward System." *Science* 188 (May 23, 1975):796-802.

Carnegie Commission on Higher Education, *Opportunities for Women in Higher Education: Their Current Participation, Prospects for the Future, and Recommendations for Action.* New York: McGraw-Hill, 1973.

Centra, John A. *Women, Men, and the Doctorate.* Princeton, N.J.: Educational Testing Service, 1974.

Darland, M.G., Dawkins, S.M., Lavasich, J.L., Scott, E.L., Sherman, M.E., and Whipple, J.L. "Application of Multivariate Regression to Studies of Salary Differences between Men and Women Faculty." In *Proceedings of the Social Statistics Section*, Washington, D.C.: American Statistical Association, 1973, pp. 120-132.

Dorfman, Robert. "Two Steps Backward: Report on the Economic Status of the Profession, 1974-75." *AAUP Bulletin* 6, no. 2 (August 1975):118-124.

Kieft, Raymond N. "Are Your Salaries Equal?" *College Management* 9, no. 23 (April 1974):23.

Lester, Richard A. "The Equal Pay Boondoggle." *Change* 7, no. 7 (September 1975):38-43.

2

Detection of Sex-Related Salary Discrimination: A Demonstration Using Constructed Data

P. Kenneth Morse

In this chapter Morse uses regression analysis to examine simulated salary data for two hypothesized schools. One is statistically and absolutely fair to professors of either sex, but the distribution is structured so that men have more years in rank, and thus the simple averages show women to be at a disadvantage. The second distribution, in which all males receive an arbitrary salary increment, is structured so that women on the average have more years in a particular rank than men, thus giving rise to simple averages that are apparently free from bias. Thus on the basis of average salary within each rank, the school that actually practiced unfair salary policies appears to have a fair salary distribution, and the school that practices a fair salary policy but whose women have fewer years in rank appears unfair.

The chapter demonstrates the power of multiple regression to look beyond simple averages of men's and women's salaries in each rank to detect the effect of sex-related salary discrimination.

With virtually every institution of higher education receiving some form of aid from the federal government (and thus subject to affirmative action requirements), the ability to identify any sex-related salary discrimination has become increasingly important. However, the very compliance with affirmative action guidelines in the employment and promotion of women may tend to increase the apparent relationship of sex to salary level, because faculty salaries are heavily determined by variables (such as rank and years in rank) that are often confounded with sex, especially where women are receiving a "catch-up" share of new appointments and promotions.

Probably the most common method of displaying salary data is by computing the mean (or occasionally the median) of all salaries within a given category. Often this is supplemented by some measure of variability, if no more than listing the highest and lowest values found in the category. This method is appropriate when the sample is large relative to the number of relevant category combinations, or cells, and when each cell is populated by an adequate subsample to provide stable cell means. However, as the number of relevant variables (and categories within variables) expands, the number of cells expands geometrically. Consider a school that employs 300 faculty of both sexes, holding three different academic ranks and three different levels of earned degree and divided into ten different departments (we will say nothing about full-time versus part-time, time in rank, research productivity, teaching skill, or any of the other considerations thought to be related to salary). This school would have to sort its 300 faculty into $2 \times 3 \times 3 \times 10 = 180$ discrete combinations of just these four variables! Clearly this is not practical. We typically see figures for mean salary by rank or by rank by sex. The purpose of this paper is to demonstrate how such means can be misleading and how the true state of affairs can be more nearly approximated by the use of multiple linear regression.

This paper has its roots early in 1977 when the University System of Georgia requested a report on sex-related salary equity from each component institution. At the Medical College of Georgia, this request was referred to the Office of Educational Research and Development, and I was asked to help design the strategy for data collection and analysis. The models previously employed in such reports were of the typical mean-salary-by-sex or mean-salary-by-rank-by-sex variety. It seemed clear that these could result in two kinds of errors: either a truly equitable situation might show up as inequitable or an inequitable situation might show up as equitable or even biased in reverse. To avoid these potential errors, we chose multiple linear regression as the method of analysis because of its ability to account for the joint effects of more than one variable.

Method

The basic approach was first to construct a staffing pattern for each of two simulated schools, with school A representing a truly fair salary situation and school B representing a systematically unfair salary situation. For the purposes of the simulation (and for the regression analysis to be reported to the University System of Georgia), "fairness" was defined as a nonsignificant increase in R^2 due to addition of the sex variable after accounting for all other relevant variables. Thus a situation in which persons of either sex with the same qualifications and experience receive the same salary (within the limits of chance variation) is considered fair.

In recent years affirmative action goals have led many institutions to increase their employment of women faculty members. Because this is a recent movement, these persons tend to be clustered in the lower ranks and at the lower experience levels within those ranks. School A, the fair salary situation, was therefore designed to reflect this pattern. School A's staffing pattern, when analyzed via the typical mean-salary-by-sex or mean-salary-by-sex-by-rank approach, tends to show women faculty members as receiving systematically less than male faculty members, when, in fact, equal salaries are paid for equal qualifications and experience.

An unfair salary situation may result from either or both of the following causes: a systematic salary bias directly attributable to sex or a systematic pattern of delayed promotion or nonpromotion of women faculty members. Clearly the combination of the two is more serious than either alone; however, on traditional analyses of mean salaries, the presence of systematic discrimination in promotion may mask the systematic salary bias. For our purposes, we decided to build both sources of bias into school B. One of the results of this decision was to create a situation in which the multiple linear regression analysis would underestimate the total sex-related discrimination in school B; this was felt to be justified for the purpose of this simulation, which was limited to demonstrating the misleading results that can be obtained from a simple analysis of mean salaries. Consequently school B (see table 2-1) was designed with a staffing pattern showing women predominantly at the upper experience levels of each rank.

The variables in table 2-1 were coded as follows for each simulated faculty member.

Variable	Name	Coding
Rank level 1	RANK1	1 if in this rank, 0 otherwise
Rank level 2	RANK2	1 if in this rank, 0 otherwise
Rank level 3	RANK3	1 if in this rank, 0 otherwise
Years in rank 1	TIME1	Number of years if currently in this rank, 0 otherwise
Years in rank 2	TIME2	Number of years if currently in this rank, 0 otherwise
Years in rank 3	TIME3	Number of years if currently in this rank, 0 otherwise
Sex	SEX	1 if male, 0 if female

Salaries were computed using the following formulas.

School A: Salary = 10,000 + 2,000(RANK2) + 6,000(RANK3) + 300(TIME1)

+ 500(TIME2) + 750(TIME3)

School B: Same formula but add + 500(SEX).

Since salaries are not usually completely determined by two or three variables, a random error was added to each salary by randomly selecting a z-score (from a table of random z-scores) and multiplying it by 1,000. Since z-scores can be either positive or negative, addition of this random error could either increase or decrease a given salary. This random error serves as a proxy for all the other unmeasured variables that help determine salary. For school A the random error had a mean of −4.58 and a standard deviation of 984.93. For school B the mean and standard deviation were 144.56 and 1,065.78, respectively. Neither mean differed significantly from zero (the expected mean of this variable).

The salaries generated by these specifications were recorded, and means and

Table 2-1
Number of Faculty by Rank, Years in Rank, and Sex: Constructed Data

Years in Rank	Rank 1		Rank 2		Rank 3	
	M	F	M	F	M	F
School A						
0	0	4	1	3	2	2
1	1	3	2	2	3	1
2	2	2	3	1	4	0
3	3	1	4	0	4	0
4	4	0	4	0	4	0
School B						
0	6	0	6	0	6	0
1	6	0	6	0	6	0
2	6	0	6	3	6	3
3	6	3	6	6	6	6
4	6	6	6	3	6	0

standard deviations were computed by school, sex, and rank. Separately by school, salary was regressed on the variables (except for random error) used in computing salary. Separate regressions were computed for each school, both with and without the sex variable. The difference in R^2 produced by adding the sex variable was tested for significance.

Results

Table 2-2 shows the mean and standard deviation of salaries by school, sex, and rank. Within schools there appears to be a difference due to sex in school A, although we saw that school A was actually free of sex-related bias. School B appears to be free or nearly free of bias, although there was a systematic bias in the computation of the salaries. Clearly the data in table 2-2 could be misleading.

The regression data, however, as shown in table 2-3, successfully detect the true state of affairs. School A is found to be free of bias ($F_{(1,113)} = 0.404$, $p > 0.10$), and school B's bias is duly noted ($F_{(1,113)} = 10.674, p < 0.005$).

Discussion

The data in table 2-2 for school A might well be typical of real institutions that have dedicated themselves to affirmative action goals by a hiring policy that seeks to increase the proportion of female faculty. Since most newly hired faculty come in at entry level, the very fact of meeting employment goals may increase the apparent discrimination in salary. Similarly the data in table 2-2 for

Table 2-2
Means and Standard Deviations of Salaries by School, Rank, and Sex

		Rank			
		Level 1	*Level 2*	*Level 3*	*All Levels*
School A:	Male	10,833	13,353	17,836	14,597
		(838)	(1,232)	(1,275)	(3,126)
	Female	10,152	12,136	16,296	11,749
		(869)	(1,052)	(1,199)	(2,386)
	Both	10,493	12,988	17,605	13,695
		(910)	(1,297)	(1,368)	(3,192)
School B:	Male	11,269	13,813	18,195	14,426
		(1,121)	(1,201)	(1,375)	(3,135)
	Female	10,965	13,016	18,450	14,031
		(1,170)	(1,167)	(1,437)	(3,270)
	Both	11,199	13,585	18,253	14,327
		(1,125)	(1,232)	(1,375)	(3,160)

Note: Standard deviations in parentheses.

school B may be typical of schools that have resisted the promotion of women to higher ranks and thereby created an apparent absence of bias when measured by mean salary levels.

Since the purpose of this paper is solely to demonstrate the superiority of the multiple regression technique over the simplistic analysis of means, rank was one of the variables used in the regression analysis. However, rank is often tainted by the same sex-related discrimination as salary; in fact, failure to promote on an equitable basis may be a major cause of salary inequity. The

Table 2-3
Effect of Adding Sex as a Predictor of Faculty Salaries

	School A	*School B*
Proportion of variance "explained" without sex as variable	$R^2 = 0.91023$	$R^2 = 0.87915$
Proportion of variance "explained" by adding sex as variable	$R^2 = 0.91055$	$R^2 = 0.88958$
Unique variance added by sex	0.00032	0.01043
F for difference between the R^2 values: Degrees of freedom = 1 and 113	0.404	10.674
Probability that this difference or a larger difference would occur by chance	$p > 0.10$ (not significant)	$p < 0.005$

regression analysis (with rank as a predictor) underestimates the total sex-related discrimination in school B. When real data are analyzed, rank and other status variables (such as departmental chairmanships) resulting from the institutional decision process should not be used in the regression analysis to determine salary equity unless they have first been tested against neutral variables and found to be free from sex-related bias.

Summary and Conclusions

Using constructed data, we have demonstrated that the commonly used method of showing mean salary by sex or mean salary by rank by sex may be misleading. An institution that is fair with respect to salaries but has recently employed significant numbers of women faculty at the lower experience levels within the various ranks will tend to appear unfair. Similarly the institution that has both a systematic sex-related bias with respect to salary and a policy of discriminating against the promotion of women faculty may appear fair or even biased in reverse! Both situations, however, are detectable using multiple linear regression analysis.

The limitations of this simulation must be kept clearly in mind. The variables employed in the simulation do not adequately measure the qualifications and productivity of faculty members. Furthermore rank itself may be the result of sex-related bias. In this simulation the bias in school B was underestimated because of this fact. Even so, the use of multiple linear regression does identify the systematic direct salary bias in school B, as well as the lack of bias at school A.

3 Salary Differences among University Faculty and Their Implications for the Future

Barbara Hauben Tuckman

This chapter examines the salary structure for full-time faculty members at universities in the United States using data gathered by the American Council on Education in a survey of postsecondary professors. The results of the study point out the differential rewards to faculty for publishing varying numbers of books and articles and for engaging in different types of activities, including teaching, research, and administration. Tuckman's findings also demonstrate the sometimes dramatic salary differences among faculty in different disciplines and with different personal characteristics, especially sex and race. The analysis not only provides an insight into some important influences on faculty behavior but also addresses the complex issue of what effects these salary differences are likely to have on faculty and higher education in the future.

The purpose of this chapter is to study the reward structure for university faculty on a nationwide basis. There are a variety of reasons that academicians are interested in studying their own system of financial remuneration, although the major reasons can probably be reduced to four. The first is that academics have been accused, rightly or wrongly, of narcissism. That is, we are egocentric in the sense that we study every aspect of our professional lives and activities, and studying our salaries is merely one piece of the larger picture. Although the goals of these detailed studies of ourselves are not always clear, it is probably an occupational hazard that we will continue to live with. Second, the study of institutions and the way they operate is intrinsically interesting to institutionalists. The academic reward structure and the decision making associated with that structure are important factors in understanding how institutions operate and how alternative policies change the reward structure.

A third reason for studying salaries is that such a study provides an opportunity to discover inequities in the existing structure, which is the first step toward correcting these inequities. The women's liberation movement has contributed to the increased interest in studying the equity of the academic salary structure. Finally, studying the reward system can tell us which activities and characteristics of faculty are rewarded and to what degree. To the extent that faculty are motivated by monetary rewards, this information will be helpful in explaining the academic incentive system and better understanding faculty behavior.

These latter two reasons have become increasingly important in recent years in light of changing economic conditions. During the 1960s when higher education was experiencing rapid growth and receiving a generous infusion of public funds, more dollars were available for all levels of operation, including faculty salaries. Concomitantly, little attention was paid to the distribution of salaries and the intricacies of the reward system. As resources began to shrink and the academic labor market tightened in the late 1960s, the growth rate of faculty salaries and faculty mobility both declined. Intense interest developed regarding the allocation of the existing salary pot and the reward system.

The logical culmination of this situation, which was intensified by affirmative action policies, was the scholarly study of salaries and the academic reward structure. For the most part these studies were of an individual institution or at best covered several institutions within one statewide system. Lack of comprehensive data has prevented systematic study of the academic salary structure on a nationwide basis. The limited data that are available cannot answer the questions of interest to the academic community. For example, the National Register of Scientific and Technical Personnel, one of the most extensive data sources available, lacks data on the number of articles and books published by faculty. This absence of data is unfortunate given the seeming importance of publications for a faculty member's career and salary.

This study attempts to fill this gap by examining the structure of salaries for university faculty on a nationwide basis. Specifically I examine the financial rewards for publishing varying numbers of books and articles and for engaging in different types of activities including teaching, research, public service, and administration, all by faculty rank. In addition, I examine the national salary structure by measuring the effects of geographic location, field, race, sex, age, and experience, again for each of the faculty ranks—in other words, the factors that influence the reward system for faculty, whether they are activities, skills, or innate or acquired characteristics. This study will provide an insight into some of the motives that influence faculty behavior. It also offers a starting point for answering the difficult question of whether this reward system is equitable.

Description of the Data

Data used in this study are from the national cross-sectional survey of faculty conducted by the American Council on Education during the 1972-73 academic year. The faculty came from 301 institutions of higher education (78 universities, 181 four-year colleges, 42 junior and community colleges) representing diverse institutional types, levels of selectivity, and amounts of institutional wealth. From an original mailing to over 108,700 individuals and two follow-up mailings, more than 53,000 faculty representing over 72 different academic disciplines responded to the ACE questionnaire. A more complete description of the design, response rate, and other characteristics of the survey and data collected may be found elsewhere.[1]

From the original ACE data file, only full-time, university faculty have been selected for this study. Part-time employees have been excluded because the reward systems for full-time and part-time faculty are not the same.[2] Similarly the study is restricted to faculty at public and private universities. The decision to limit the analysis to university faculty is based on the realization that the system of rewards differs by type of institution. Extensive analysis of the data reveals that a better-developed reward structure exists at universities than at two- and four-year colleges.[3] Exclusion of the latter two types of institutions from this study implies, not that their reward systems are less interesting, but that they are more difficult to identify.

It would be prohibitively expensive to analyze all the academic disciplines in the original ACE data file, not only because of the size of the data file but also because one of the objectives of this study is to undertake individual within-field analyses. Therefore twenty-two fields were selected from the initial seventy-two for inclusion in this paper. The new sample was constructed to include representative fields from each of the major disciplines, groups including the biological, health, physical, and social sciences; education; engineering; fine arts; the humanities; and law. Excluded were faculty from agriculture, business, home economics, library science, physical education, and social work. The selective nature of the data file suggests that the results of this analysis are not applicable to all disciplines but only to fields included in this study. The new data file consists of 15,238 faculty of which 6,967 (45 percent) are full professors, 4,504 (30 percent) are associate professors, and 3,767 (25 percent) are assistant professors.[4]

Methodology: Variables in the Model

The purpose of this study is to examine the existing reward structure in academe to better understand some of the factors that may influence faculty behavior. The model proposed in this paper integrates productivity factors, faculty activities, and other personal and job-related characteristics into a salary estimation model. The results of the analysis should also make it possible to comment on the equity of faculty salaries.

The method used in this chapter is straightforward. Ordinary least-squares regression is used to quantify the direct effects of faculty activities and characteristics on salaries. Institutional salary is the dependent variable. The several independent, explanatory variables were selected on the basis of previous work in this area. They include number of articles and books published, sex, race (black or white), highest degree completed, years of experience, years of experience squared, age, age squared, prime work activity (currently in administration, previously in administration, research, teaching), nine-month or eleven- or twelve-month contract, regional location of employment, and field of specialization.

Equations are estimated separately for faculty in each of the assistant, associate, and full professor ranks and for faculty from all the ranks combined. Faculty member's salary, the dependent variable used in the regression, consists solely of the income received by a faculty member from the employing institution. Outside income such as consulting fees and royalties not derived from the faculty member's institution is excluded because the focus of this study is on the reward structure at the universities. The independent variables affecting salary are dummy variables, except for the age and experience variables. The intercept term includes white, female economists on nine-month contracts, engaged in teaching, without a Ph.D. or other doctoral degree, and located in the West-Southwest.[5]

The publication variables are not discrete. Rather the variables for numbers of articles and books published by faculty are broken into interval categories. The number of articles published is partitioned into intervals of 1-2, 3-4, 5-10, 11-20, 21-50, and 50 or more articles, with each interval represented by a dummy variable that assumes a value of 1 when the number of articles published by the faculty member falls into the corresponding group and 0 otherwise. Books are broken into four groups, 1-2, 3-4, 5-10, and 10 or more, with a dummy variable assigned to each. The same 0-1 criterion is used. The publications variables are broken down because of the way the survey was conducted. The ACE questionnaire asked that faculty check the appropriate article and book interval categories rather than list the actual number of articles and books they had published. Therefore discrete variables could not be used to estimate the effects of the number of articles and books published on faculty salaries.[6]

A further difficulty is that data are not available on the quality of the journal that a faculty member publishes in or on the quality of that person's books. Because of this, a direct adjustment for quality cannot be made.[7] Thus these estimates may measure returns to quantity rather than quality of publications. There is evidence that quantity and quality may be correlated.[8] However, it is not clear that article quality enters directly into the reward structure through the publications variable. Rather it may enter indirectly by increasing the opportunities for faculty to move to institutions offering higher salaries or to obtain an administrative or research position.

A faculty member's work activity is classified into administration, teaching, and research. This grouping is determined from the faculty member's response to a survey question asking about his or her major work activity. The survey also inquired about previous work in administration. Past administrative activity is based on the faculty member's response to questions asking whether he or she has ever held a universitywide administrative position or been a departmental chairman. Dummy variables are constructed for all these variables. The contractual period of employment indicates either a nine-month contract or an eleven- or twelve-month contract. A dummy variable is assigned a value of 1 for the eleven- or twelve-month contract, and the nine-month contract is included in the intercept term of the equation.

The Ph.D. variable is used to represent highest degree and denotes whether a person has a Ph.D., L.L.B., M.D., D.D.S., or Ed.D. degree. A dummy variable with a value of 1 is included to indicate whether the faculty member is black. If the faculty member is white, the variable is included in the intercept. Similarly a dummy variable is assigned a value of 1 if the faculty member is male, and the female variable is in the intercept.

Dummy variables are also constructed for the location of the faculty member's institution to allow for regional differences in the reward structure. Dummy variables are set up for the North, Great Lakes, and South; and a value of 1 is assigned to the dummy when an institution is located in the corresponding region. The Southwest and West regions are combined in the intercept term.

Age is measured by chronological age, and experience is defined as the number of years from the time a person receives his or her highest degree to the 1972-73 academic year.[9] Previous studies in this area indicate that age and experience have a nonlinear effect on income.[10] After experimenting with several nonlinear forms of these two variables, I decided to include a squared term for each of the variables to capture these nonlinearities. By a nonlinear effect we mean that income does not increase proportionately as age and number of years of experience increase. Rather, income increases by greater than or less than a proportional amount. Squaring each of the age and experience variables enables us to determine whether these variables cause salary to increase at an increasing or a diminishing rate through time.

Dummy variables are set up for each of the disciplines. The appropriate variable is assigned a 1 depending on the faculty member's field. Economics is included in the intercept term. Since salary levels seem to be partially dependent on the faculty member's field, it is important to adjust for field differences.

The System of Rewards to Faculty

The regression results are shown separately for each of the faculty ranks and for the all-ranks-combined equation in table 3-1. For each of the four regression equations, the coefficients are shown for the independent variables discussed in the previous section.

Table 3-1
Model Coefficients by Rank

Independent Variable	Full Professor	Associate Professor	Assistant Professor	All Ranks
Number of Articles				
1-2	646	382	415[b]	484[a]
3-4	768[a]	667[a]	579[a]	786[a]
5-10	1,788[a]	867[a]	474[b]	1,357[a]
11-20	2,360[a]	1,208[a]	756[a]	2,169[a]
21-50	3,411[a]	1,514[a]	635	3,375[a]
50+	5,539[a]	2,450[a]	2,918	5,992[a]
Number of books				
1-2	305[a]	197	96	386[a]
3-4	749[a]	454[a]	543	996[a]
5-10	1,419[a]	376	253	1,713[a]
10+	880[a]	255	689	1,200[a]
Work activity				
Research	1,146[a]	520[a]	287	506[a]
Current administration	3,397[a]	2,561[a]	2,282[a]	3,251[a]
Past administration	1,627[a]	585[a]	538[b]	1,787[a]
Eleven-month contract	3,176[a]	2,442[a]	2,035[a]	2,634[a]
Region				
North	1,348[a]	1,443[a]	720[a]	1,065[a]
Great Lakes	860[a]	530[a]	517[a]	717[a]
South	641[a]	1,109[a]	516[a]	620[a]
Personal Characteristics				
Male	1,410[a]	1,165[a]	724[a]	1,143[a]
Black	1,457[a]	1,009	1,975[a]	1,799[a]
Ph.D.	1,008[a]	416[b]	197	1,570[a]
Age	666[a]	482[a]	357[a]	669[a]
Age squared	−7[a]	−5[a]	−4[a]	−7[a]
Experience	227[a]	50	101[a]	243[a]
Experience squared	−1[a]	−2[b]	−3[a]	−2[a]
Fields				
Anthropology	−2,728[a]	−1,128[a]	−2,068[a]	−2,601[a]
Biochemistry	−2,356[a]	−554	−1,217[a]	−2,652[a]
Botany	−4,418[a]	−2,559[a]	−1,663[a]	−4,082[a]
Chemistry	−2,522[a]	−1,770[a]	−1,654[a]	−2,900[a]
Civil engineering	−1,275[a]	−343	−514	−908[a]
Earth science	−2,769[a]	−1,457[a]	−1,220[a]	−2,585[a]
Education	−2,822[a]	−1,551[a]	−906[a]	−2,448[a]
Electrical engineering	−338	−428	−294	−526[a]
English	−2,047[a]	−2,340[a]	−2,583[a]	−2,665[a]
Geology	−2,995[a]	−1,918[a]	−1,845[a]	−2,824[a]
History	−1,336[a]	−1,925[a]	−2,385[a]	−2,000[a]
Law	3,575[a]	1,717[a]	804	2,867[a]
Mathematics	64	−434	−921[a]	−689[a]
Medicine	5,541[a]	7,870[a]	8,420[a]	5,243[a]
Music	−3,265	−2,406[a]	−2,802[a]	−3,226[a]
Pharmacy	−3,476[a]	−452	288	−2,375[a]
Physics	−1,376[a]	−1,104[a]	−1,204[a]	−1,827[a]

52814

Table 3-1 continued

Independent Variable	Full Professor	Associate Professor	Assistant Professor	All Ranks
Political science	−1,070[a]	−1,104[a]	−1,474[a]	−1,373[a]
Psychology	−1,869[a]	−1,273[a]	939[a]	−1,900[a]
Sociology	−1,419[a]	−1,017[a]	−1,064[a]	−1,413[a]
Zoology	−4,239[a]	−2,306[a]	−1,694[a]	−3,937[a]
Constant	−3,859[b]	1,747	4,221[a]	−5,570[a]
Adjusted R^2	0.49	0.48	0.37	0.59
Standard error	4.69	3.54	4.27	4.48

[a]Coefficient for this variable is significant at a 5 percent level.

[b]Coefficient for this variable is significant at a 10 percent level.

Book and Article Publication

The results of the regression equation concerning direct salary rewards to faculty who publish journal articles are quite interesting. Faculty members who publish articles receive sizable salary increments relative to their counterparts who do not publish, and the greater the number of articles, the greater the salary reward tends to be. For instance, a full professor with three to four articles earns $768 more than a full professor with no publications; for a full professor with fifty or more articles, the differential is $5,539. Similar results are found for the all-ranks equation and the associate professor equation, although the rewards earned by associate professors are smaller than those earned by full professors. An associate professor earns $667 more than a nonpublishing counterpart for three to four articles and $2,450 more for fifty or more articles. The pattern for the assistant professor regression is less clear-cut, and the coefficients for the 21-50 and 50+ categories are not significant. One explanation may be that assistant professors do not remain in their rank long enough to publish a large number of articles.

For the most part, however, faculty seem to be well-rewarded financially for article publication. Given that faculty are motivated by financial rewards,[11] one would expect to find academics engaged in publishable research and writing. Two points should be noted. First, article quality is not considered here. This does not imply that faculty are rewarded purely on the basis of number of articles published; quality was not considered only because this analysis cannot differentiate on that basis. Second, article publication is also rewarded financially, albeit indirectly through promotion to a higher rank and thus a higher salary.[12] This analysis, again, does not measure such indirect rewards.

The relationship between book publication and direct salary rewards is considerably less clear-cut. The relationship is not significant for assistant and associate professors. For full professors and for all ranks combined, the salary rewards increase as the number of books published increases up to the 5-10 interval, and then they drop off in the 10 or more category. However, the direct monetary rewards involved appear to be considerably less than those for article publication. A full professor who has published ten or more books, for example, receives only $880 more than one who has published no books. One explanation may be that books do not represent the same scholarly achievement that articles seem to and therefore bring a smaller reward.

Although book publication seems to bring some financial rewards, we might question whether the costs associated with book publication are not greater than the returns. If costs are greater than returns, faculty may be less motivated to engage in book publication given the size of the direct salary rewards. (Book publication, like article publication, may be rewarded indirectly through promotion to a higher rank.) There may be other direct rewards, however, that this analysis does not capture. Since the salary variable is measured net of any outside income, faculty may be receiving royalties for book publication. Alternatively, the lure of large and continuing royalty checks from an introductory textbook that has large adoptions may induce faculty to take the gamble and expend considerable time and effort to write textbooks. Another possibility is that the direct salary rewards may be small in absolute terms but relatively large in terms of effort expended, since some types of books such as edited readings or collections of essays merely involve bringing together the writings of others. If this analysis could distinguish by type, length, and quality of books, we might find that the direct salary rewards vary significantly.

Other Work-Related Characteristics

In addition to publications, a variety of other work-related characteristics brings rewards to faculty. Primary work responsibility is one. Faculty whose major work activity is research earn an average of $506 more than faculty engaged primarily in teaching. The associate professor engaged in research earns $520 more than his teaching counterpart, and the full professor researcher earns $1,146 more.[13] These differentials are likely to be even greater if the publication variables are removed from the regressions, since researchers are more likely to publish than teachers. These results are not surprising. Although teaching may be emphasized at some institutions, the rewards often go to those who engage in research and publish. One explanation is that it is more difficult to evaluate (and therefore reward) good teaching than research. Also, while good teaching is important, it does not bring the same recognition and prestige to departments and institutions that research can. Thus to the extent that faculty are motivated by financial rewards, we would expect to find those currently in teaching moving in the direction of research and publishing, and those already doing so to continue.

For faculty whose primary work is administration, the rewards are substantial. The faculty member in administration earns an average of $3,251 more than the faculty member in teaching.[14] Full professors in administration receive $3,397 more than their teaching counterparts, and associate professors earn $2,561 more. Even for the assistant professor regression, where the coefficients tend to be smaller than for the other three regressions, the differential is a substantial $2,282. Since administrators are frequently employed on eleven- or twelve-month contracts, the rewards for administration can be considerably greater than these figures indicate. Of course, one might argue that the duties and responsibilities of administrators in higher education today are so demanding that these financial increments are relatively small. On the other hand, for some academics, moving into administration may be the best or perhaps the only way to substantially augment their salaries. While a full professor could receive an equal reward either by being an administrator or by publishing twenty to fifty articles, the latter might take twenty or more years to accomplish!

Faculty members who were previously in administration also receive financial rewards. The increment is $538 for the assistant professor, $585 for the associate professor, and $1,627 for the full professor. This differential exists primarily because salary increments received by faculty while in administrative capacities are sometimes retained when they return to teaching or research positions. Faculty members going into administrative positions for a couple of years with the primary goal of raising their salary base need to be aware, however, that many institutions are changing their policies and giving salary supplements to faculty only during their administrative tenure. Furthermore, where collective bargaining has been adopted or where there are moves toward salary equalization schemes, faculty with previous histories of administrative activity are on the firing line for their high salaries, and some even seem to be in danger of losing their increments.

Thus while faculty currently engaged in administration receive fairly large rewards for their activity, it appears that the rewards are in recognition of the different type of effort put forth. Since many administrators are required to keep long and regular office hours, some of the supplement could simply be a reflection of more hours and not higher wages. Administrators may also be rewarded for their willingness to give up the opportunity to become consultants or researchers. For some faculty the reasons for becoming an academic would be lost in the administrative work, and salary rewards of these magnitudes are unlikely to induce different behavior. Since faculty stepping down from administrative posts are now less likely to retain their supplements, even fewer faculty may be willing to assume administrative burdens. This is especially true in view of the decline in enrollment growth and funding for higher education, which tend to make administrative roles considerably less desirable. However, administration can offer a viable and attractive alternative for faculty who, having proven their "worth" in academia, do not really want to spend the rest of their careers teaching, doing research, and publishing.

As we might expect, regional location of the faculty member's institution has an effect on the reward structure. In each of the four regressions, faculty receive the greatest reward if they are at a northern institution and the smallest if they are in the West and Southwest (combined in the intercept term). Except at the associate professor level, those in the Great Lakes receive more than those in the South. While it is not surprising that northern faculty receive the largest rewards, we might have expected to find the lowest increments in the South where salaries and the cost of living tend to be the lowest in the country. Although faculty may be motivated to migrate north in search of higher salaries, it is possible that this regional pattern may be changing. With demographers projecting the greatest population growth in the South and Southwest through the 1990s, we may find relatively greater expansion of higher education in these regions with correspondingly larger salary rewards. Whether much expansion in higher education will occur at all is questionable, however, with the traditional college-age population expected to level off nationwide. Finally, the large increment to associate professors in the South may reflect a phenomenon of the tight academic labor market in the late 1960s when southern institutions were offering higher salaries to attract new Ph.D.'s from highly rated graduate schools. At the time of the survey this group was likely to be found at the associate and assistant professor levels.

Personal Characteristics

Different personal characteristics bring varying rewards to faculty. For the most part faculty have little or no control over these characteristics, so we are not concerned with whether rewards to these variables will influence behavior. What we are concerned with, however, is whether personal characteristics over which one has no control are rewarded differently. This, then, raises the question of salary equity.

Sex. Male faculty members on the average earn $1,143 more than female faculty. Being male brings a salary reward about equal to that for publishing ten or more books. A male assistant professor earns $724 more than a female assistant professor, a sizable increment to this rank, while a male associate professor is rewarded $1,165 more than his female counterpart. In both cases the reward for being male is about the same as the reward for publishing eleven to twenty articles. At the full professor level the differential is $1,410. These results, of course, are not unexpected. The interesting thing is that these differentials would probably be greater if the analysis had included disciplines in which a majority of women are employed and which tend to be lower paying.

In the past many female faculty have been denied the opportunities to engage in research and other activities that are rewarded financially and increase one's chances for promotion. Female faculty are often given heavier teaching loads, more student advising, and heavier committee assignments than their male counterparts. They are less likely to be assigned graduate assistants and generally tend to receive less overall support for scholarly endeavors than their male colleagues. A further explanation for the differential is that women are sometimes less mobile than men, and in the past it has been harder for women to change jobs. Both factors tend to depress female salaries relative to those of males. These are just a few of the many possible explanations for the inequality of male and female faculty salaries. From this analysis it is not possible to discern whether female faculty are being discriminated against by receiving lower salaries than their male counterparts or whether they are receiving lower salaries based on the work they perform, which may be a result of past or current discrimination or of choice. In either case, there is cause for concern, and future studies need to address this issue.

Whatever the cause of these unequal salaries, the situation has been changing, although very slowly. The women's rights movement, along with the appointment of affirmative action officers on many campuses, has led to salary equalization programs for female faculty.[15] The adoption of collective bargaining on some campuses has also led to salary equalization schemes. Finally, changing attitudes toward the employment of women and the realization that women have the ability and desire to perform the same functions as men have helped to change the situation somewhat, especially for younger women entering academe. It will take many years, however, for female faculty to move up through the ranks and reach equality with male faculty at the full professor level where the number of females is small, both relative to the other ranks and in an absolute sense, and the salary differentials are great. Thus we would expect the differentials to decrease through time but at a fairly slow pace.

Race. Like sex, race also brings different returns, and the differential for race is even greater than that for sex, except at the associate professor level where the coefficient is not significant. The black faculty member receives an average of $1,799 more than his white counterpart, while the sex differential is only $1,143 in the all-ranks regression. The black assistant professor is rewarded $1,975 more than the white assistant professor. This increment is the largest of the four regressions, and it is more than 2½ times the sex differential at the assistant professor level.

A possible explanation for the large race differentials in all four equations is that affirmative action and equal employment opportunity programs at many universities have encouraged the hiring of more black faculty. However, with such a limited pool of black faculty or blacks with the requisite credentials, universities must often offer above-average salary levels to attract black faculty. Also black faculty can often command higher salaries than their white counterparts because they tend to have higher opportunity costs[16] given the big demand for them in private industry and the public sector. These two factors also explain why the differential is greatest at the assistant professor level: university competition at the assistant rank tends to reflect changes in supply-and-demand phenomenon more rapidly than at the higher ranks. A variety of equal educational opportunity programs have recently enabled more qualified blacks to attend undergraduate and graduate school, so the largest pool of available black faculty are young Ph.D.'s at the assistant level. These differentials may decrease as more blacks attend graduate school. However, the pool of qualified blacks is still small relative to the demand for them, and graduate school involves several years, so the process of adjustment in the marketplace may be a slow one. These differentials are therefore likely to persist for some time.

Some have argued that affirmative action policies are merely a fad of the 1970s and that the interest in salary and employment policies for females, blacks, and other minorities will fade quickly. It is probably true that the intensity of interest in these areas cannot remain at its present high level, but it is likely that affirmative action policies are here to stay. Once the initial interest has been aroused and the affected groups realize that employment policies can be fair and equal, they will continue to bring public interest and legal pressure to their cause.

Other Personal Characteristics. Age and experience have important effects on the academic reward structure. The age and experience variables each have the greatest effect at the full professor level and the smallest effect at the assistant level. Within each of the ranks the contribution of these variables to salary diminishes as a faculty member grows older. In the all-ranks equation the relationship between age and salary peaks at the age of forty-nine and declines thereafter. In the individual equations the peaks range from age forty-nine for associates to age forty-seven for assistants. The returns to experience do not peak until well beyond retirement age. Since the effects of age dominate those of experience, the results suggest that after age forty-nine increasing age results in negative salary increments, measured on a cross-sectional basis.[17] This finding is consistent with age-earnings profiles for the professional fields.[18]

Degree held is a personal characteristic over which a faculty member has control. The faculty member holding the Ph.D. or highest degree in his field receives an average reward of $1,570 more than his counterpart without the degree. This result is not surprising, because faculty are often hired at different salary levels depending on the degree held. The full professor with highest degree is rewarded $1,008 more than his counterpart without the highest degree. Thus holding the highest degree is rewarded more highly than publishing three to four articles or books at the full professor level. While this might suggest that earning the highest degree is a worthwhile option, the situation differs at the associate and assistant levels where the increments are absolutely and relatively less. This is partially an indication that a larger percentage of faculty in the lower ranks have the highest degree. In fact, in many cases it is a prerequisite for the position. Thus although earning the highest degree may seem less worthwhile at the lower ranks, it may be a necessity. Note that the coefficient for the assistant level is not significant.

The Different Disciplines

Since economics is included in the intercept term, each of the different discipline variables indicates the financial differential between that discipline and economics for each of the four regressions. For example, a full professor of anthropology receives an average of $2,728 less than a full professor of economics. The most interesting feature of the field coefficients is the overwhelming number of disciplines in which faculty receive less than economists. The two main exceptions are law and medicine, where faculty members earn more than economists at each of the ranks and in the all-ranks equation. In medicine the differentials are substantial, going as high as $8,420 at the assistant professor level. These findings suggest that salary differentials among fields are determined to a large extent by opportunity cost factors. Obviously, since medical doctors can earn very high salaries in private practice or at least outside academe, their opportunity costs are quite high, and these are reflected in their academic salaries. Likewise, lawyers who choose to teach can leave academe and earn a higher salary in private practice. Economists have far more job opportunities in government and private industry than historians, anthropologists, and English majors, for example, and this is reflected in lower salaries for these three fields.[19]

For the most part these differentials are quite large, with the absolute amounts tending to be greater at the full professor level than at the assistant level. For example, a full professor of education receives $2,822 less than his counterpart in economics, while an assistant professor of education receives only $906 less than an assistant professor of economics. For botany the respective differences are −$4,418, and $1,663; for earth science, −$2,769 and −$1,220; for geology, −$2,995 and −$1,845; for zoology, −$4,239 and −$1,694. While this tends to be the general pattern, there are a few exceptions such as political science, medicine, English, and history, where the differential at the assistant professor level is greater than at the full professor rank.

Music faculty receive considerably lower salaries than economists. This is probably because music faculty, like art faculty, often teach at universities to assure a steady stream of income while continuing to pursue their profession on the outside. The psychology differential is positive at the assistant professor rank and then becomes negative at the associate professor and full professor levels. This may be a reflection of a slightly different labor market for psychologists than for other academics because more outside opportunities tend to be available to new Ph.D.'s. Similar reasoning may apply to the unusual pattern for pharmacy faculty, although the coefficients for the assistant and associate ranks are not significant.

The varying rewards to the different fields are fairly substantial in most instances, a fact that seems to substantiate the common argument that the academic labor market is broken into separate submarkets by field. This division is due largely to the fact that there is virtually no movement between fields because faculty skills are so highly specialized. Thus these differential rewards, although large, are unlikely to influence faculty to change fields. The situation may be different for graduate students, who might be motivated to change fields because of these differentials. It is unlikely that an English major would switch to economics purely for monetary incentives, but it is very likely that a student interested in economic history might switch from history to economics for financial rewards. Since these differentials are actually reflections of varying opportunity costs, the graduate student's behavior may be influenced more by outside opportunities than by salary differentials.

Implications for the Future

The results of this study clearly indicate that certain activities and characteristics of faculty are more highly rewarded than others, with dramatic differences in some cases. Publication brings large rewards, with publication of articles bringing larger returns than publication of books. The rewards for article publication increase substantially with the number published. These results are not unexpected, of course, since anyone familiar with the current academic scene is aware of the publication syndrome. By way of contrast the returns to faculty engaged in administration are about 50 percent as great as the returns received by faculty publishing fifty or more articles, while faculty engaged in teaching receive lower salaries than either researchers or administrators. The differences between administrators and other faculty are even greater when consideration is given to the fact that a higher percentage of administrators are on an eleven- or twelve-month contract. The regional location of employing institutions also brings varying returns.

The returns to the personal characteristics variables are interesting, although not entirely unexpected. Male faculty receive an increment above female faculty in each of the ranks and for all ranks combined. While the differentials are not as great as for some of the other variables, the other differentials appear more justified by rational causes. Black faculty get a larger return than their white counterparts at each of the ranks, and the differential at the assistant professor level is very high. Opportunity costs seem to be an important factor in this case. While the effects of aging differ according to rank, in each rank aging has a negative effect on salaries beyond age fifty. This result is consistent with other studies. Finally these results suggest that the returns to the various disciplines vary substantially according to field and rank. Opportunity costs and the fact that faculty possess highly specialized skills seem to account for these differentials.

This system of rewards applies only to universities. It is not difficult to imagine that the rewards would be substantially different at a two-year college, for example. While a seasoned publisher at a university is more highly rewarded than a colleague who excels in teaching and interacting with students, a person actively engaged in research at a two-year or community college may not receive normal salary increments if his or her teaching and student advising suffer as a result of research. Furthermore public service, especially community activities, may be rewarded differently at the two institutions. Whereas this activity might be of minor importance in the role of a university faculty member, it could be a requisite for employment at a two-year community college. Finally the salary rewards among fields at two- and four-year colleges and universities would be substantially different, because the demand for and emphasis placed on various fields of specialization vary greatly among institution types. Thus the existence of these and other differences in the reward structure at various institutions points out the importance of examining only one type of institution instead of aggregating the data.

Now that faculty as well as administrators and legislators are becoming more aware of which activities and characteristics are rewarded the question is, What will happen? Will this information merely be acknowledged and ignored? Will it affect individual faculty behavior? Or will it cause structural changes?

On an individual level greater knowledge of the salary structure is likely to have some effect on faculty behavior, although large-scale changes are not likely. Rather this knowledge is more likely to influence the faculty member's allocation of time. In view of the finding that publishing numerous articles can raise salaries over time, some faculty may place more emphasis on publishing. We might expect to see faculty devoting less time to teaching and more to research and publishing, because those who publish appear to earn more than their unpublished peers, even though the returns may exceed the costs. It also seems reasonable to assume that nondirect financial returns in the form of promotion, mobility, and wider career options, which bring their own returns, increase the returns to publication still further. Faculty may also be more motivated to move into administrative work, not only for the larger reward, but also to gain the longer contractual period of employment which eliminates the need to scramble for summer funding. Evidence of the differential returns to the race and sex variables may lead to more lawsuits and legal appeals by individuals. On the other hand, women may be more motivated to allocate their time and resources to activities that bring greater returns, such as research and publishing.

On an aggregate level these differentials may be used to help spur the adoption of collective bargaining and union demands to reduce differences among faculty through a single salary structure. Even if collective bargaining is widely adopted at universities, some differentials will continue to exist among different fields because of the likelihood that some disciplines will form their own associations and remain outside the bargaining unit. This is particularly likely to occur in the professional fields such as medicine, law, and engineering. However, in the academic fields we may find a leveling process by which the salaries of less productive faculty and those in lower-paying fields are raised to the average level. If this happens, the more productive faculty who have a large number of outside opportunities and are not receiving adequate salary increments may leave academia or move to institutions where their efforts will be rewarded. The danger of this possibility is compounded by the fact that faculty salaries have been losing ground relative to other occupations. Unfortunately, if the better faculty leave academia, higher education in the United States may become mediocre.

Another problem that awareness of salary differentials is leading to is the movement by state legislators to mandate greater emphasis on and recognition to teaching. Certainly the teaching function at universities is important and should not be overlooked. Unfortunately increased emphasis on teaching may occur at the expense of research, which is a major function of most American universities. It is often argued that good teaching goes along with and is a product of research. Thus legislative mandates regarding teaching might induce top faculty to leave the universities and thus interfere with the orderly discovery and transfer of knowledge.

As institutions of higher education face increasing pressure from declining enrollments and reduced federal and state funding, the demand for faculty is likely to decrease. It seems crucial, then, to attempt to hire and retain the best faculty possible. One good way to achieve this is to allow the academic labor market to function freely, without interference, and to make sure that faculty are rewarded, not just for performing their jobs, but for engaging in productive activities.

Notes

1. A.E. Bayer, *Teaching Faculty in Academe: 1972-73* (Washington, D.C.: American Council on Education, 1973).

2. H.P. Tuckman and W.D. Vogler, "The 'Part' in Part-time Wages," *AAUP Bulletin* 64 (May 1978):70-77.

3. H.P. Tuckman, *Publication, Teaching, and the Academic Reward Structure* (Lexington, Mass.: Lexington Books, D.C. Heath, 1976).

4. The actual number of fields represented in the ACE data file depends on the researcher's definition of a separate field. For example, some psycholo-

gists treat clinical and experimental psychology as separate fields. In choosing representative fields, we were governed by a desire to include all the social sciences to permit further analysis of within-field differences. The other disciplines were chosen by reference to the number of faculty in the data file, the representativeness of the field, and the extent to which this field is taught at a wide range of universities in the United States.

The twenty-two fields include anthropology, biochemistry, botany, chemistry, civil engineering, earth science, economics, education, electrical engineering, English, geology, history, law, mathematics, medicine, music, pharmacy, physics, political science, psychology, sociology, and zoology.

The ACE data file consists of 19,493 full-time university faculty of which 8,984 are full professors, 5,803 are associates, and 4,706 are assistants. From this subpopulation, 22 percent of the cases were eliminated because values for one or more variables were missing. A t-test of the means suggests that the elimination of these values did not significantly change the character of the original data file.

5. Dummy variables are used to represent qualitative variables, such as sex or race, and groupings of quantitative variables, such as age and income intervals. In our study, for example, female = 0 and male = 1. For each observation, if the faculty member is male, the sex variable assumes a value of 1 and the female variable appears in the intercept term. The interpretation of the full professor male dummy variable of $1,410 (see table 3-1, full professor column) is that male full professors earn $1,410 more, on the average, than their female counterparts.

6. Use of interval variables enables us to capture nonlinearities in the data. Unfortunately the nature of the intervals makes it difficult to identify diminishing returns to additional publications.

7. Much work needs to be done before such an adjustment is possible. Problems exist in providing for differences in articles due to length, content, and joint authorship. These issues are explored by A.E. Bayer and J. Folger in "Some Correlates of a Citation Measure of Productivity in Science," *Sociology of Education* 39 (Fall 1966):381-390.

8. S. Cole and J.R. Cole, "Scientific Output and Recognition: A Study in the Operation of the Reward System in Science," *American Sociological Review* 32 (June 1967):377-390.

9. The highest degree might be Ph.D., M.D., Ed.D., J.D., and so forth. Alternatively, it may be M.A., M.S., M.M., M.F.A., or even B.A. Experience is measured from the point when formal schooling appears to have been terminated. It might be argued, however, that some faculty remain in school beyond the time when they receive their highest degree but eventually leave without completing the next degree. We are unable to determine whether this has an effect on our estimates, although past studies suggest that those who do not complete a degree do not receive the salary increases that those who complete that degree receive.

10. G.E. Johnson and F.P. Stafford, "Lifetime Earnings in a Professional Labor Market: Professional Economists," *Journal of Political Economy* 82 (May/June 1974):549-570; G.E. Johnson and F.P. Stafford, "The Earnings and Promotion of Women Faculty," *American Economic Review* 64 (December 1974):888-904; and N.A. Tolles and E. Melichar, "Studies of the Structure of Economists' Salaries and Income," supplement to *American Economic Review* 58 (December 1968), part 2.

11. Tuckman, *Publication*.

12. H.P. Tuckman and J. Leahey, "What is an Article Worth?" *Journal of Political Economy* 83 (October 1975):951-98.

13. Another study finds that outstanding teaching is worth less than a good publication record. See J.J. Siegfried and K.J. White, "Financial Rewards to Research and Teaching: A Case Study of Academic Economists," *American Economic Review* 53 (May 1973):309-316.

14. In their study of professions listed in the National Register, Tolles and Melichar find that work in management raises faculty salaries 17 percent above the salaries of those in research and 27 percent above those in teaching. See Tolles and Melichar, "Economists' Salaries and Income."

15. For some examples of these, see chapter 5-8, in this book.

16. Opportunity cost refers to the price that a faculty member could earn in his or her next best alternative use. The opportunity cost of an engineer, for example, would be considerably greater than that for a historian specializing in the history of the Danish railway system. This is a useful concept that we will refer to later in this chapter.

17. A common finding in studies of age-earnings profiles is that earnings decline as the faculty member ages. When time-series data are employed, however, the results suggest that earnings continue to rise at a diminishing rate.

18. G. Becker, *Human Capital* (New York: Columbia University Press, 1964).

19. The approach adopted here assumes that the dummy variables for the individual fields capture the among-field differences. For a more complete approach see Tuckman, *Publication*.

4

A Generalized Multiple Regression Model for Predicting College Faculty Salaries and Estimating Sex Bias

Glenworth A. Ramsay

This chapter develops a general model of multiple regression prediction of salary and discusses some of the pitfalls of multicollinearity, proxy variables, specification error, and simultaneous equation bias. In the second part the author applies the analysis to a random sample of the 1972 ACE data dealt with by Barbara Tuckman in chapter 3.

It is intuitively obvious that when two people, one male and one female, have the same qualifications and perform the same job at different salaries, there is sex discrimination. In the past this idea was used in an attempt to detect discrimination. The salary of a woman was compared to the closest matched male (counterpairing). Unfortunately in the academic world many factors can be considered legitimate determinants of salary—rank, publications, experience. It is often impossible and always debatable to find a pair that are closely matched. For that reason universities are turning to regression analysis, a more sophisticated and less heuristic approach, to detect discrimination.

Appropriate use of the technique involves two and sometimes three steps. The first step requires development of a mathematical model, or equation that describes a set of factors that the institution uses either implicitly or explicitly to determine salaries. The second step applies ordinary least squares to estimate the coefficients or weights of the factors implied by the data. The third step uses the resulting equation to calculate the salary of a fictitious person (predicted or fitted value) that matches the individual in all relevant factors. The predicted and actual salaries are then compared, and conclusions are then drawn as though the counterpairing technique were being used.

Most studies of salary inequities have emphasized the second and third steps with little or no attention to the first. This is unfortunate, because the value of regression analysis depends critically on model development, and model development has a substantial impact on the subsequent steps. Estimation of the parameters applies a sophisticated but relatively value-free technique, but this step is predicated on a properly specified model, which is not and cannot be developed in a value-free setting. Moreover an improperly specified model can easily result in biased estimates.

The first part of this paper quickly reviews the type of ad hoc modeling or crude empiricism that is typical of most salary inequity studies based on regression analyses. It then describes in detail some of the resulting statistical and interpretation problems. The second part develops and estimates an alternative model of salary discrimination. The data for the estimation stage are a random sample of the data from the 1972 American Council of Education survey of over 53,000 faculty members throughout the United States. The purpose of the random sample is to simulate a university of 250 faculty members.

Ad Hoc Modeling or Crude Empiricism

Virtually all salary inequity studies use cross-sectional data. That is, the data consist of information on all full-time faculty members of the institution in a given year. Because it is a cross section, as opposed to a time series, the data reveal nothing about the mechanism that causes the distribution of salaries. This is of central importance because the interpretation of the results now rests entirely on the model itself. Precisely the same results may be consistent with two models, one that implies discrimination and one that does not.

The crude modeling that is done usually consists of selecting from the available data variables that are believed to affect salary either directly or indirectly with very little concern about how or why these variables are important. A second, but equally thoughtless technique, uses stepwise regression in which the final set of variables are defined as those that worked the best. This is simply building the model that fits the data, a suspicious and logically incorrect procedure.

Four potentially serious statistical problems are likely to result from ad hoc modeling. The first is multicollinearity. The probability that multicollinearity reaches an objectionable level increases with the number of variables included in the analysis. The second is the use of proxy variables to reflect concepts that are not directly observable. This problem is closely related to multicollinearity. The third is specification bias, a problem that arises when an important variable is omitted from the analysis. The fourth is simultaneous equation bias in which a simple single-equation model not only abstracts from reality but also distorts it.

Multicollinearity

The right-hand-side variables in a regression equation are usually called independent variables. They are independent in the mathematical sense that one variable can be changed without changing any of the other independent variables. They are not necessarily independent in the statistical sense. Observations on two right-hand variables may in fact be highly (but not perfectly) correlated.[1]

Although multicollinearity does not violate any of the assumptions of regression analysis, it increases the standard errors of the estimated coefficients and may lead the investigator to conclude that something is insignificant when it is in fact quite significant but its effect is spread across variables.

For example, if research productivity and sex are both included in the model and are strongly correlated with each other, it becomes difficult to separate their individual effects. Ordinary least squares reveals this essentially logical difficulty by producing large standard errors on both coefficients. Part of the effect of research will be attributed to sex and vice versa, making the estimated individual effects unreliable. To omit the variable causing the collinearity solves the problem but guarantees a specification bias problem. The only satisfactory solution to the collinearity problem is to obtain more information. However, we are assuming that the investigator is dealing with the most complete data set available; hence obtaining more information is nearly impossible.[2]

Without further information the multicollinearity problem requires careful and often subjective interpretation. In this example, where research and sex are multicollinear, a significant t-statistic on the sex coefficient indicates a statistically significant salary differential based on sex. On the other hand, if the t-statistic is not significant, the multicollinearity problem prevents the investigator from concluding that the salary differential due to sex is statistically insignificant.[3]

One of the most controversial multicollinearity problems occurs in universities that contain female-dominated colleges such as nursing or home economics. If department or discipline is included, it is quite likely that the t-statistic on sex will be insignificant. This is partially due to multicollinearity. If department or discipline is then dropped, the coefficient on sex becomes significant. The argument is often made that women are being forced into the lower-paid disciplines and deliberately excluded from the higher-paid disciplines. This is tantamount to arguing that salary discrimination is being "enforced" through a mechanism of discipline selection. If this were the entire mechanism, discipline and sex would be so highly correlated that either sex or discipline would contain all the explanatory power. In other words, one variable or the other is redundant. This extreme form of multicollinearity is fairly easy to detect; three regressions, one containing sex but not discipline, one containing discipline but not sex, and one containing both, will all have approximately the same R^2, but the third will have insignificant t-statistics on both the sex and discipline coefficients.

Unfortunately the situation is seldom so obvious. There is some collinearity but also some individual explanatory power in both sex and discipline. Careful modeling is essential if one hopes to clarify the problem. Several models are capable of explaining these results, and choosing between them is a subjective judgment. The two extreme models can be labeled the Marxist and capitalist models. The Marxist model argues that sex discrimination is present both in discipline selection and in salaries within discipline. Either women are forced into low-paid disciplines, or disciplines that are predominantly female are deliberately underpaid. There is discrimination both directly and indirectly; including both variables simply masks the extent of the discrimination, and the collinearity problem makes the t-statistic on sex insignificant. People should be paid according to how much they work—a forty-hour week in home economics is the same as a forty-hour week in accounting. Discipline is not a legitimate determinant of salary and should be omitted from the regression; the coefficient on sex will then pick up both sources of discrimination, precisely what is being measured.

The capitalist model argues that people should be paid according to the value of their work. Value is reasonably measured by salaries paid in the market. The fact that accountants are paid substantially more than home economists simply means that society's demand (relative to supply) for accountants is substantially greater than the demand for home economists. Academic salaries must be high enough to attract people from alternative employment; hence the professor of accounting is quite legitimately paid more than the professor of home economics. It is therefore necessary to include discipline to capture the effect of these legitimate market forces.

Both models have merit. Both are internally consistent and both explain the empirical findings. However, the two models yield radically different policy conclusions. Further research on different data is needed to differentiate between the two models. Why are higher-paid disciplines dominated by males? Is it tradition? Will salaries and sex distribution adjust as market forces work themselves out? Is there some institutional or sociological impediment to women who wish to enter these fields? Once these questions have been answered, it is possible to consider what policy should be adopted and at what level that policy can be implemented.

Is it a department, university, academic, or national problem? These are extraordinarily important questions, but they cannot be answered with the cross-sectional data used in university salary differential studies. I believe that the questions can be dealt with only by estimating a disequilibrium labor market model. To estimate such a model, long-time series data are necessary but currently unavailable.

Multicollinearity is often treated as a minor statistical problem and not cause for worry. However, when multicollinearity is viewed not as a statistical problem but as a modeling problem, one cannot seek refuge in the robustness of regression analyses. The estimates obtained by ordinary least squares are still unbiased, but the conclusions and interpretations are radically altered in the presence of multicollinearity.

Proxy Variables

An issue closely related to multicollinearity is the use of proxy variables. Proxy variables are used when data do not exist for the actual concept the investigator wishes to include in the model. A proxy variable is simply a variable that is believed to be highly correlated with the actual concept and for which data exist. The problem with proxy variables is that it is impossible to test whether the variable is a good proxy, that is, whether it is highly correlated with the actual concept. Furthermore, it is possible that the variable is not really a proxy but belongs in the model on its own merit. In this case the proxy variable and the actual concept have some independent effects, but to include both (if this were possible) would clearly cause a collinearity problem. Proxy variables are most often used in salary inequity studies when the investigator is attempting to include things such as experience or skill as legitimate determinants of salary. That experience and skill are determinants of salary is unquestioned; indeed, they are the basis of the rank system.

Although experience is conceptually easy to measure and is undoubtedly used in the individual bargaining process for starting salaries, it is not a variable that is commonly and clearly found in personnel data. Experience is thus proxied by such measures as years since terminal degree or age. Both proxy variables are clearly correlated with experience, but neither is perfectly correlated. Although years since terminal degree is a reasonable proxy for experience, it is really a minimum measure. It is quite possible that an individual's experience exceeds years since terminal degree but unlikely that it is less. This means that years since terminal degree does not reflect average experience but something less. This failure of a proxy to precisely measure the actual concept is important when the regression equation is applied to individuals in the third step of the process.

On the other hand, using age as a proxy for experience errs in the opposite direction—experience cannot possibly exceed age but can be varying amounts smaller. Of more importance is the possibility that age may have a separate effect. An individual's salary should increase with experience, as his or her services become more valuable to the university. As the individual gets older, he or she may become more tied to a particular area and hence lose bargaining power. These are very separate effects and deserve to be measured independently. Unfortunately using years since terminal degree as a proxy for experience and age as a direct measure often results in a severe multicollinearity problem that produces insignificant t-statistics on both concepts.

Specification Error

One of the assumptions of regression analyses is that the disturbance term is independent of each and every independent variable.[4] There are two situations in which this assumption is likely to be violated. The first is specification error—omitting an important variable. The second is simultaneous equation bias. In both cases standard regression analyses (ordinary least squares) will produce biased estimates of the coefficients.[5]

A biased estimate is simply incorrect; its distribution is not centered on the true value, and any statistical test of its validity is therefore invalid. Again the initial cause of both specification and simultaneous equation bias is improper modeling.

Including all possible variables is likely to result in multicollinearity and subsequent misinterpretation of the significance of some of the variables. The problem can be alleviated by including fewer variables, but omitting an important variable, even if it is statistically insignificant, can cause biased estimates of the coefficients of the remaining or included variables. The extent and direction of this bias depends on the correlation between the omitted and included variables.

For example, suppose that salaries are determined by research and teaching and that women are underpaid. Because of the difficulty of quantifying teaching, the investigator decides not to include it in the equation. Figure 4-1 shows the results of excluding teaching under various assumptions about the correlation between teaching and sex. The solid lines in each of the three panels represent the true relation between salary and research under the assumption that the quality of teaching is identical for all individuals. The dots represent observations for males, the crosses represent observations for females. In the two panels in which the correlation between teaching and sex is nonzero, the dashed line represents the estimated relationship for women.[6]

If the correlation is zero, that is, teaching ability is unrelated to sex, the estimated and actual relationships will be as close as statistically possible. Teaching, although it is a determinant of salary, is randomly distributed across both sexes and therefore appears as part of the disturbance term—a poor teacher is just as likely to be a male as a female. The argument is often made that any missing variable is simply "picked up" by the disturbance term and including it would merely increase the R^2 by removing part of the cause of observations deviating from the line. This is certainly true in the first panel where the correlation between sex and teaching is zero, but it is only partially correct in the remaining two panels.

If teaching and sex are positively correlated, that is, women are generally superior teachers, then the part of the disturbance term due to this missing variable will tend to be more positive than negative. This situation is depicted in the second panel. The true relation is predicated on equal teaching, but the superior teaching of women is reflected in higher salaries. The effect of omitting teaching when it is positively correlated with sex is to mask the effect of discrimination: the estimated differential in salary is much less than the actual differential.

If women are generally inferior teachers, the correlation between teaching and sex will be negative. This results in a tendency for the disturbance term to be negative, as in the third panel. The estimated relation accentuates the discrimination in salary. The effect of omitting a variable not only lowers the predictive power of the model but may have a substantial effect on the estimated effect of the included variables.

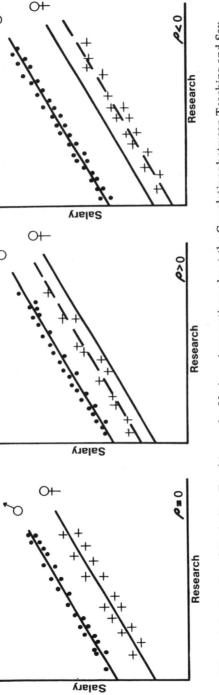

Figure 4-1. Results of Excluding Teaching under Various Assumptions about the Correlations between Teaching and Sex.

While this explanation may seem intuitively obvious, correlation chains can become quite complex. Consider the same situation with no correlation between teaching and sex but a positive correlation between research and sex, with the men being the more prolific researchers. Figure 4-2 shows the results of various correlations between research (the included variable) and teaching (the omitted variable).

If research and teaching are positively correlated, the women (less research) will appear to be underpaid (because their teaching is poorer). Conversely, if research and teaching are negatively correlated, the discrimination will once again be masked. Note that in this case the coefficient on research (the slope) has also been biased.

The effect of omitting a variable depends on a variety of correlations. If the omitted variable is correlated with any one of the included variables, any or all coefficients may be biased. Given that very little in the world is really independent, specification bias due to omitted variables is of great concern.[7] This does not imply that proper modeling include all variables. It does imply that the investigator should be reasonably confident that the variables omitted from the model are uncorrelated with the included variables. Often variables are omitted because they are difficult to quantify; in this case a caveat is in order when interpreting the results.

Simultaneous Equation Bias

The omission of a variable may easily violate the assumption that the disturbance term and the independent variables are uncorrelated. This same assumption is quite likely to be violated when ordinary least squares are used to estimate an equation that is actually part of a simultaneous system. The violation has the same disastrous consequences—biased estimates of the coefficients. Whether an equation is part of a simultaneous system depends purely on the model.

The problem can be explained by the salary-discipline-sex entanglement introduced in the discussion of multicollinearity.

The Marxist and capitalist models could be combined and better represented by a two-equation model. The choice of discipline depends on salary (the capitalist argument) and sex (the Marxist argument) and is modeled by equation 4.1.

$$DISC = \alpha SAL + \beta SEX + \eta \qquad (4.1)$$

where η is a random disturbance term.

Salary is determined strictly by discipline (including SEX does not alter the argument but unnecessarily clutters it) and is modeled by equation 4.2.

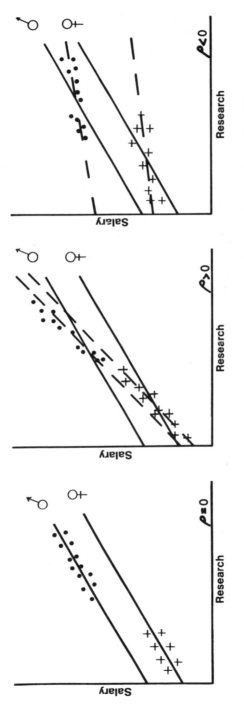

Figure 4-2. Results of Various Assumptions about the Correlations between Research and Teaching.

$$SAL = \gamma + \delta DISC + \epsilon \qquad (4.2)$$

where ϵ is a random disturbance term.

The disturbance term in equation 4.1 is clearly related to DISC, the variable on the left-hand side. Unfortunately equation 4.2 now guarantees that that relationship will be fed through to SAL, which is a right-hand variable in equation 4.1. Hence one cannot argue that the disturbance term and the right-hand variables in equation 4.1 are independent.

Whether one estimates equation 4.1 or 4.2, the problem persists; the estimated coefficients will be biased. The traditional single-equation model (salary as a function of both discipline and sex) has no relation to the two-equation model, and one cannot draw any conclusions about the two-equation model from estimating the traditional model.

A strikingly similar situation exists more when one considers rank. It is often argued that discrimination exists more in the promotion process than salary; that is, women are retained in rank longer than men. This reasoning requires a two-equation model, one for salary and a second for rank.

$$SAL = \alpha + \beta RANK + \epsilon \qquad (4.3)$$

$$RANK = \gamma + \delta EXP + \lambda SEX + \eta \qquad (4.4)$$

where EXP is some variable reflecting experience. This model is recursive and does not cause all the difficulties of the previous model. Although equation 4.4 feeds back into equation 4.1 through rank, the converse is not true. Unlike the previous model, there is no reason for the disturbance term in equation 4.4 to be related to either of the right-hand variables.[8] For this reason, ordinary least squares can be applied to equation 4.2 but not to equation 4.1. Once again, the traditional single-equation model including both rank and sex bears no relation to the two-equation model.

Model building plays an important part in regression analysis. Choosing the variables that belong in the model can have serious consequences, both for obtaining unbiased estimates and for interpreting the results. Including too many variables increases the likelihood that multicollinearity will cause the investigator to misinterpret the results. Too few variables almost certainly causes specification bias in which ordinary least squares produces biased estimates of the coefficients. The use of proxy variables can easily cause both problems. The way that the variables enter the model, whether in single equation or in a system of equations, can cause biased estimates of the coefficients. Techniques such as two- and three-stage least squares are designed to alleviate this bias. However, if a single-equation model is used to represent a situation that can be better represented with a multiequation model, there is bound to be confusion and misinterpretation.

An Alternative

The purpose of this section is to develop an alternative model that differs in several important respects from the traditional model. The most important difference is that it is a two-equation model specifically designed to deal with the salary-rank conundrum discussed in the previous section. The first equation determining salary is more carefully developed and directly tied to a national price index. The second equation, used to determine rank, explicitly allows for sex discrimination in the promotion process.

Because the model will be estimated using data from the 1972 American Council of Education survey, the variables have been restricted to those available from the ACE survey and, at the same time, easily accessible from university personnel files. The two restrictions mean that the model is considerably simpler (and hence more unrealistic) than would be the case if only one restriction were imposed. Starting rank and the timing of promotions are available in most personnel records and would allow much more detailed modeling of the rank equation. Furthermore the ACE data are national and therefore reflect a variety of regional differences that would not be present in a single university study. The random selection of 250 individuals is meant to simulate a university; hence regional variation is not modeled.

Derivation of the Salary Equation

An individual's current salary (1972 in this case) is based on a series of historical incidents. It is difficult to model such a phenomenon from cross-sectional data alone. However, with some simplifying assumptions a reasonable attempt can be made. An individual's salary in year t is by definition the sum of the starting salary and all subsequent increments:

$$SAL_t \equiv START_r + \sum_{i=r}^{t} INCR_i \qquad (4.5)$$

where r is the year hired at the institution. The subscript t is always 1972, so it will be dropped. Probably the overriding determinant of starting salary, $START_r$, is the year the individual began work at the institution. This is not a factor unique to educational institutions; it is merely a result of economywide inflation. The inflation rate has not been constant, so it cannot be properly modeled by a time trend of any sort. This factor is explicitly included in the model by using the annual consumer price index. The two remaining legitimate factors contributing to starting salary are peculiar to academic institutions; they are discipline and starting rank. Finally, many argue that sex discrimination occurs for a variety of reasons during initial bargaining sessions. The last three variables, discipline, starting rank, and sex, are all qualitative variables and are entered as a series of shift or dummy variables.[9]

$$START_r = \alpha + \beta CPI_r + \sum_{i=1}^{N} \gamma_i \, DISC_i + \sum_{i=1}^{3} \delta_i \, SRANK_i + \theta SEX \qquad (4.6)$$

The increment in salary during any one year i is based on a cost-of-living increase and an increase based on promotion.

$$INCR_i = \alpha_1 \Delta CPI_i + \sum_{i=1}^{3} \phi_j \, PROM_j \qquad (4.7)$$

Clearly a host of other variables are important, though the data limitations make them difficult to include. Summing equation 4.6 over the years of employment at the institution yields

$$\sum_{i=r}^{1972} INCR_i = \alpha_1 \sum_{i=r}^{1972} \Delta CPI_i + \sum_{i=r}^{1972} \sum_{j=1}^{3} \phi_j \, PROM_j \qquad (4.8)$$

Assuming, as seems reasonable, that an individual can be promoted to a given rank only once and is not promoted twice in one year, then one can rearrange equation 4.8 and write it in the following way:

$$\alpha_1 \sum_{i=r}^{1972} \Delta CPI_i + \sum_{j=1}^{3} \phi_j \sum_{i=r}^{1972} PROM_j \qquad (4.9)$$

Substituting equations 4.8 and 4.6 into equation 4.5 and rearranging terms yields

$$SAL = \alpha + \beta CPI_r + \alpha_1 \sum_{i=r}^{1972} \Delta CPI_i + \sum_{i=1}^{N} \gamma_i DISC_i + \sum_{i=1}^{3} \delta_i SRANK_i$$

$$+ \sum_{i=1}^{3} \phi_i \sum_{j=r}^{1972} PROM_j + \theta_1 SEX \qquad (4.10)$$

This equation can be simplified, first by algebraic manipulation of the terms involving the CPI and second by assuming the premium paid for the various ranks is the same whether it is a starting rank or a promotion ($\delta_i = \phi_i$). The result is

$$SAL = \alpha' + \beta' CPI_r + \sum_{i=1}^{N} \gamma_i DISC_i + \sum_{i=1}^{3} \delta_i \left(SRANK_i + \sum_{i=r}^{1972} PROM_j \right) + \theta_1 SEX$$

$$(4.11)$$

where $\alpha' = \alpha + \alpha_1 CPI_{72} > \beta' = \beta - 1$. The term in parentheses, starting rank plus promotions, is simply current rank.

The final equation for determining salary is

$$SAL = \alpha' + \beta' CPI_r + \sum_{i=1}^{N} \gamma_i DISC_i + \sum_{i=1}^{3} \delta_i RANK_i + \theta_1 SEX \qquad (4.12)$$

Derivation of the Rank Equation

The second equation of the model determines rank. It would be of particular interest to model rank through the promotion process, but the ACE data do not contain information about the individual's history through the rank system. This equation contains four legitimate determinants of rank: experience, which is proxied as years since terminal degree (YSTD); publication of articles; publication of books;[10] and Ph.D. or equivalent.

Finally, SEX is added to allow for discrimination in promotion procedures. Expressed in general notation, the RANK equation is

$$RANK = f(YSTD, PUB1, PUB2, PHD, SEX). \qquad (4.13)$$

Equation 4.13 poses a difficult methodological problem; RANK is not a continuous variable, nor is it a quantitative variable. There is a growing body of literature (most notably Daniel McFadden's "Conditional Logit Analyses of Qualitative Choice Behavior," in *Frontiers of Econometrics*) that suggest that equations such as 4.13 can be estimated using the individual-specific multivariate logit. The logit estimates the probability that an individual with the characteristics described by the right-hand variables will hold a given rank.[11]

Estimation of the Model

The model is composed of equation 4.12, which determines salary, and equation 4.13, which determines rank. It is a recursive model in which equation 4.13 determines rank purely from exogenous variables. Once rank has been determined, the predicted rank can be combined with the remaining variables in equation 4.7 to determine salary. For this reason, the results of estimating equation 4.6 will be discussed first.

The individual specific logit produces a set of coefficients with associated
t-statistics for each rank. The coefficients are normalized in the same way that
dummy variables are used in regression analyses; that is, they measure the
importance of the associated variable relative to the omitted rank, in this case,
instructor. Table 4-1 presents the estimated coefficients for assistant, associate,
and full professors.

There are no particular surprises in the legitimate determinants of rank. The
only variable of significance at the rank of assistant professor is possession of the
Ph.D. degree. At the rank of associate professor experience and the publication
of books also became significant. The publication of articles is insignificant and
not of the expected sign. One strongly suspects that this is due to multicollinearity. Finally, at the rank of full professor all legitimate determinants of
salary are significant and of the correct sign.

The sign of the coefficient associated with the sex variable indicates
discrimination against women at all ranks, although it is statistically significant
only at the associate level. This could easily be interpreted as discrimination in
the tenure process. The coefficient is roughly the same for both the assistant and
associate levels, but it falls dramatically at the rank of full professor. There are a
variety of explanations for this pattern, ranging from "Female full professors in
1972 must have been truly outstanding" to "The sample size is too small to risk
interpretation."

To estimate and avoid simultaneous equation bias in the salary equation, the
actual rank must be replaced; with the predicted rank from equation 4.13. The
coefficients from table 4-1 are used to calculate the probability of each of the
three ranks for each individual. The logit guarantees that the probabilities for all
four ranks will sum to one; hence the probability of instructor is one minus the
sum of the probabilities of the three remaining ranks. The predicted rank is then

Table 4-1
The Estimated Coefficients of the Rank Equation

	Assistant	Associate	Full
Intercept	0.368	0.077	0.126
	(2.87)	(0.80)	(1.42)
Experience	0.005	0.021	0.009
	(0.52)	(5.11)	(2.95)
Publication of articles	−0.005	−0.0039	0.056
	(−0.16)	(0.18)	(3.19)
Publication	0.118	0.117	0.042
	(1.31)	(2.78)	(1.54)
Degree	0.377	0.511	0.382
	(4.59)	(8.46)	(6.03)
Sex	0.135	0.134	0.083
	(1.40)	(1.82)	(1.01)

Note: t-statistics in parentheses.

simply the rank with the highest probability. Once the predicted rank has been substituted for the actual rank in the data, ordinary least squares can then be applied to equation 4.13 without the risk of bias. The results are presented in table 4-2.

Both discipline and rank are series of dummy variables, so the intercept of $6,850 represents the salary of an instructor in the humanities. The coefficient on the price index indicates that starting salaries through 1972 have more than kept pace with inflation; this result is disappointing for those who feel that continuing salaries have not, but they can take comfort in the fact that it is insignificant. The series of dummy variables associated with discipline are weak and difficult to explain. This weakness is undoubtedly due to regional differences in the data, and one would expect an actual university to show considerably more robust results. The coefficients associated with the predicted ranks are significant and are consistent with a priori beliefs.

The sign of the coefficient associated with sex indicates discrimination against women. The t-statistic indicates this discrimination is significant at the 90 percent, albeit not the 95 percent, confidence level. To emphasize the importance of simultaneous equation bias, the equation was reestimated using actual instead of predicted rank. There was a slight decrease in the sex coefficient from 1.12 to 1.07 and a decrease in the t-statistic from 1.6 to 1.32. This second estimate is akin to the single-equation ad hoc modeling criticized earlier in this chapter. The conclusions that the investigator would reach depend very much on the underlying model.

The two-equation model indicates that there is significant discrimination in the promotion of women from assistant to associate professor. By substituting

Table 4-2
The Estimated Coefficients of the Salary Equation

Variable	Coefficient	t-Statistic
Intercept	6.85	(3.19)
CPI_r	2.10	(1.23)
Disciplines		
Business	0.33	(0.35)
Engineering	0.44	(0.39)
Science	−0.15	(−0.23)
Social science	0.55	(0.68)
Education	1.52	(2.14)
Predicted rank		
Assistant	1.57	(1.60)
Associate	4.87	(4.90)
Full	9.88	(9.58)
Sex	1.12	(1.60)
$R^2 = 0.48.$		

the predicted rank for the actual rank, one can see the effect of sex on salary for equally qualified people no matter what their actual rank might be. The discrimination in salary is significant. When actual rank is used, the significance of the sex variable vanishes.

The two-equation model reveals discrimination in terms of both promotion and salary, yet the single-equation model indicates no discrimination in salary and is incapable of detecting discrimination in promotion. The discrimination in promotion is clearly biasing the coefficient on sex in the salary equation. This bias is downward so that women who are underranked do not appear to be underpaid. The important point is that careful modeling not only produces different results from the same data but also sheds more light on the process of discrimination.

Conclusion

This alternative model clearly demonstrates the pitfall of simultaneous equation bias, yet it is subject to its own pitfalls. Probably the worst is specification bias due to omitted variables. If the model were applied to an actual university, it would necessarily have to be adapted to include variables and concepts that that university considers important for promotion. The idea that one can simply use a prepackaged model is dangerously naive. The numerical results of regression analyses are objective and value-free, yet those results and their interpretation are crucially determined by the underlying model.

Notes

1. The Gauss-Markov assumptions require the matrix of $K + 1$ right-hand side variables to be of full column rank. This is necessary and sufficient to guarantee $K + 1$ independent normal equations. This assumption is met even if several of the off-diagonal elements of the correlation matrix are very high. It is violated if they are strictly equal to 1.0 in absolute value.

2. Ridge regression is said to solve the multicollinearity problem. However, ridge regression is essentially a Bayesian technique in which the additional information is merely the investigator's a priori beliefs.

3. This situation is different from the fact that insignificance means that "one fails to reject the null hypothesis." While that is a disappointingly weak statement, in the presence of multicollinearity one is not really justified in going even that far.

4. The relevant Gauss-Markov assumption is that X, the $K + 1$ matrix of independent variables, is nonstochastic. This assumption implies $E(X\epsilon) = \emptyset$, where ϵ is the vector of disturbance terms. The assumption of independence,

$E(X\epsilon) = 0$, is a weaker assumption that still allows one to prove that the ordinary least-squares estimates are unbiased.

5. The word *bias* is being used strictly in the statistical sense that the expected value of the estimate is equal to the true value.

6. We are assuming that sex enters the equation as a shift variable where SEX = 1 if female, 0 if male; hence, it is the female relationship that appears to move relative to the male.

7. This is one of the major difficulties with stepwise regression. A variable may be omitted from the final form because it is insignificant, yet its omission biases the remaining coefficients.

8. DISC is, of course, not a continuous variable and would have to be estimated using a discrete-choice algorithm such as the multivariate logit. Or it could be measured as the number or proportion of new entrants in a particular discipline, in which case equations 4.3 and 4.2 represent a host of equations, one for each discipline.

9. Experience is an exogenous variable in this model and probably rightly so. With a few notable exceptions, SEX is predetermined by the time an individual chooses a career.

10. The two types of publications reflect the format of the ACE data; in neither case is there any attempt to measure quality.

11. The logit specifies each rank as

$$R_i = \exp(B_i X) / \overset{J}{\Sigma} \exp(B_j X)$$

where X is a vector of variables and B_i is a vector of associated coefficients. R_i is therefore defined on the 0-1.0 range. The B's can be estimated using any maximum-likelihood procedure.

Part II
Case Studies in Salary Equity at Representative Institutions

5

Effects of Statewide Salary Equity Provisions on Institutional Salary Policies: A Regression Analysis

Mary P. Martin and
John D. Williams

This chapter examines the consequences of salary equity provisions in North Dakota. It is a fascinating application of the multiple regression procedure, particularly because the salary equity issue was embroiled in the statewide allocation of salary monies to each of three kinds of institution: two-year institutions, state colleges, and universities. The state system was interested in retaining an appropriate differential in average salary between them and did so on the basis of differential allocation of salary increases.

As institutions of higher education complete equity studies and actually award differential increases based on these studies, a natural question arises regarding the effect that such increases have on institutional salary policies. Of considerable importance is monitoring any change in the institutional salary structures; of particular interest is measuring any change in the importance of teaching, research, and service. Also of interest is the effect of equity increases on sex differences regarding salaries.

Several different units could constitute the faculty included in an equity study. While many institutions will opt for a study in which the faculty of the institution constitute the group to be studied, larger or smaller units can also be considered. One study of interest would encompass all faculty under a statewide board of higher education. When all faculty at several different institutions under a single state board are involved in an equity study, an additional question that should be addressed is the possibility of change in a single institution's salary policies when the equity study is completed on a multi-institution basis. This latter concern is addressed in this chapter regarding a statewide equity study in which monies were actually distributed to faculty.

Background

The state of North Dakota supports eight institutions of higher education: two universities, four state colleges, and two two-year institutions. There has been a long history of disagreement over the average faculty salary figure used in the state formula to allocate salary monies to the three kinds of institutions. The state board of higher education has in the past supported the philosophy of retaining a differential, for example, a $2,000 difference between the two-year institutions and the universities and a $1,500 difference between the state colleges and the universities. If a 6 percent salary increase is given to university faculty and if the differential is maintained at the same dollar level, faculty at the other type of institutions would receive salary increases in excess of 6 percent. Salary increases for all state employees were set at 6 percent by the state legislature, so it became necessary to resolve the two conflicting policies.

A solution to this conflict in policies was pursued with the intent of implementing equal pay for equal work. The amount for the biennium that would normally establish the differential was $228,776. An appropriation of $228,776 was made to be used by the state board of higher education for the purpose of creating more equitable salary authorizations to the institutions and addressing primarily the aforementioned objectives.

Setting the goal of equal pay for equal work does not define the mode of accomplishing that ideal. Undoubtedly some observers would prefer that any such equity money be allocated on some preferential basis by which a target group (women, professors of undergraduates, nontenured faculty, or highly successful researchers) is allocated a much larger share to address presumed systemwide defiencies. Others might wish to isolate personnel who have similar duties at different institutions and run several separate studies. Such approaches to addressing inequity are interesting, but a process using multiple linear regression with all faculty in a statewide system is described here.

Statewide Model

All full-time faculty ($N = 984$) at state institutions of higher education are included. Variables included six categorical variables reflecting years of experience at the current institution, four variables reflecting highest degree, four rank variables, highest program level of department (graduate, undergraduate, associate), and twenty-one Higher Education General Information Survey (HEGIS) classifications. No traditional outcome variables (research, teaching, service) are included. These variables were excluded for what one might describe as political considerations. Only the two universities place any importance on research; the remaining six institutions felt it unfair for them to be compared in an equity study to university faculty who were expected to be more productive in research than other faculty.

The committee responsible for conducting the equity study could not agree on the teaching and service variables. The state college members wished to include number of hours of teaching per week (a move that would favor the state colleges, since faculty at the state colleges have more teaching hours per week). The two university committee members preferred a measure of student credit hours produced (a move that would favor the universities because there are much larger classes at the universities). In the end no measure of teaching was agreed on; neither of the proposed measures directly assessed quality of teaching. Because no outcome variables were included, detractors might claim that an elaborate salary scheme has been devised in which a person's salary is determined entirely by rank, teaching field, degree, program level, and years of experience without regard to the success or failure of the individual.

Results of the Committee's Analysis

Inequity was initially defined to be a negative residual. Thus if a person's salary exceeded the predicted salary, resulting in a positive residual, no inequity was seen to be present. For each institution the sum of negative residuals was found (but using an overall statewide equation). The total sum of negative residuals, $670,339, obviously exceeded the allocated amount. Each institution was then accorded a share of the total amount in relationship to its proportion of the total sum of negative residuals. Then 25 percent of the amount to be allocated to the two universities was reallocated to the remaining six institutions; the reasons for the 25 percent devaluation of university "inequities" reflect the compromises of the committee more than any statistical consideration. Because the dollar amount was equal to a presumed underpayment of nonuniversity faculty, members of the committee from the other institutions felt they had a better claim on the equity money. One pitfall to consider in equity studies is the importance of political considerations. Even the choice of the variables to be included is to some degree political; no research, teaching, or service measures were included in this statewide study. Also of importance is the makeup of any decision-making group. Having one member on the committee from each institution makes it seem as if each member represents the employing institution. Thus several committee members may see themselves in the advocacy position of attempting to gain as much as possible for their home campuses. In such a light, holding the group strictly to the initial task may be somewhat illusory. Additional details of the committee's deliberations can be found in Williams and Martin (1977).

In the final analysis the University of North Dakota was to receive $51,624 for the biennium for "equity" pay. State-board guidelines included the following.

1. The university will commit 48.5 percent of its allocation the first year of the biennium.
2. Distribution will be made only to individuals with negative residuals.

3. No individual will receive more than his or her negative residual.
4. Faculty representation is necessary in the distribution process.

Additional provisions that the University of North Dakota attempted to use included the following.

5. All equity monies would be distributed to colleges within the university in proportion to their present salary expenditures without regard to the residuals in the statewide equation.
6. Most available monies were to be given to professors and associate professors. Only if insufficient faculty at higher ranks were available with negative residuals would assistant professors be considered for equity adjustments.
7. In any case only those considered especially meritorious should be given equity adjustments.

The guidelines contain sufficient incongruities to insure that they were not always applicable. The vagaries of the regression process insured some interesting adjustments. Because those at higher ranks will tend to have higher salaries and hence are less likely to have negative residuals, the most likely recipients are those few higher-ranked individuals who have a comparatively low salary. In at least some cases the lower comparative salary probably reflected lower productivity than their same-ranked colleagues. The question then arises, What effect on the overall faculty salary structure, particularly as it reflects outcome variables (research, teaching, and service) do the equity adjustments cause?

Research Design

All full-time tenured or tenure-track faculty wholly funded on 1977-78 appropriated monies on whom complete data were available were included in the sample. The independent variables are recorded in table 5-1. The dependent variables were the 1977-78 contracted salary and the 1977-78 salary after the equity adjustment. The zero-coded variables were instructor, sociology, 0-2 years of experience, and undergraduate degree offered in home department and a holder of a master's degree. The research variable was a measure used at the University of North Dakota; while many idiosyncrasies are involved, ten points on the research variable represents publication as a single author of an article in a refereed journal of national or international status. Other types of publication are covered as well. An average for the past six years was used as the measure of research productivity; if the faculty member had less than six years of professional activity, then the appropriate number of years was used in the averaging process. The teaching variable is the mean rating of the faculty member by students in the most recent administration of the rating scale. Seven faculty did not have a rating, reducing the population from 319 to 312. The

Table 5-1
Variables Included in the Regression Analysis Regarding Equity
Adjustments to Salaries at the University of North Dakota

Variable	Variable Number	Coding[a]
Degree level	2	Doctorate
	3	Bachelor's
	4	Professional
Years experience at	5	3-7
current institution	6	8-12
	7	13-17
	8	18-22
	9	Over 22
Level of program and contingent research involvement	10	Graduate program
Sex	11	1 if male, 0 if female
Discipline	13	Biological sciences
(HEGIS taxonomy)	14	Business and management
	15	Communications
	16	Computer and information sciences
	17	Education
	18	Engineering
	19	Fine and applied arts
	20	Foreign languages
	21	Health professions
	22	Home economics
	23	Law
	24	Letters
	25	Mathematics
	26	Physical sciences
	27	Psychology
Rank	28	Professor
	29	Associate professor
	30	Assistant professor
Research	31	Publications
Teaching	32	Teaching rating
Service	33	University senate
(university committees)	34	Elected committees
	35	Senate committees
	36	Presidential committees
	37	Appointed committees

[a]All categorical variables except sex were coded 1 for *yes*; 0 for *no*.

service variable was assessed as the number of years served on five different kinds of university committees: the university senate, committees elected on a university wide basis, committees elected by the university senate, committees appointed by the president, and other appointed committees; ad hoc committees were not included. Committee memberships for the past five years were included.

Results

Tables 5-2 and 5-3 report the results of using the independent variables; these tables respectively report the results for the 1977-78 contracted salary and the 1977-78 salary after the equity adjustments.

Table 5-2 reports salary determinations that took place at the University of North Dakota before any involvement (or knowledge) of the equity process; thus it can be seen as reflecting the priorities (even as they are changing) in the salary determination process before the intervention. The question that arises regarding table 5-3 is whether the intervention (equity) process has changed to any significant degree in the salary determination process.

This question can be answered directly by imposing the regression coefficients established in table 5-2 plus the mean increase $75.19 to the data set that formed table 5-3 using the following (Ward and Jennings, 1973) equation.

$$F = \frac{(q_2 - q_1)/(df_1)}{(q_1)/(df_2)}$$

where q_1 is the sum of squared deviations from the regression line for table 5-3 and q_2 is the sum of squared deviations for the imposed equation. The F-test in this circumstance tests the ability of the preequity equation to predict post-equity salaries. The resulting F-value is within rounding error of zero, indicating a close fit to the preequity equation.

While considerable difficulty is encountered in trying to interpret each coefficient in the tables, the following directions of change can be noted from table 5-2 to table 5-3: the research and teaching variables appear to have minimal importance in the salary determination process (from the correlation coefficients, the regression coefficients, and the beta weights). On the other hand, being on the university senate was associated with having a higher salary. A variable included in the analyses that fairly does not belong is sex. It is included as a control variable; because discrimination is being attended to on a national level, the variable may have some predictive value due to efforts to eliminate discrimination. The drop in the size of the coefficient for sex from table 5-2 to table 5-3 seems to indicate a slight move toward addressing this issue. Were the salaries actually nondiscriminatory, the regression coefficient for sex would be zero. It appears that the greatest attention is focused on rank, degree level, and some of the HEGIS categories, notably law. Using the degree variables, rank variables, and six HEGIS categories (management, computer and information sciences, education, fine and applied arts, foreign languages and law), a total of twelve variables, results in only a minimal drop in the R^2, from 0.83333 to 0.81421, if salary after the equity adjustment is the criterion. Using rank and the HEGIS category for law (a total of four variables), $R^2 = 0.74206$, amounting to slightly more than a 9 percent drop in accounted variance despite the elimination of thirty-one variables.

It can be argued that the reason the outcome variables have so little impact in complex equations such as those demonstrated in tables 5-2 and 5-3 is that

Table 5-2
Multiple Regression for Equity Study before Adjustments for
Faculty at the University of North Dakota
(n = 312)

Variable	Mean	Standard Deviation	Correlation with Salary	Regression Coefficient	Computed t-Value	Beta
Ph.D.	0.657	0.475	0.360	1050.36	4.299	0.145
B.A.	0.012	0.112	−0.147	545.67	0.604	0.017
Prof.	0.006	0.079	0.068	3203.01	2.577	0.074
3-7 years	0.240	0.428	−0.028	121.17	0.387	0.015
8-12 years	0.275	0.447	0.069	151.87	0.447	0.019
13-17 years	0.134	0.341	0.085	359.17	0.891	0.035
18-22 years	0.051	0.220	0.127	915.37	1.736	0.058
Over 22 years	0.080	0.271	0.173	695.57	1.428	0.054
Grad. prog.	0.868	0.338	0.076	88.02	−0.277	−0.008
Sex	0.855	0.351	0.267	390.88	1.307	0.039
Biol. sc.	0.044	0.207	0.116	−154.80	−0.300	−0.009
Bus. & man.	0.105	0.308	0.061	1794.89	4.724	0.160
Comm.	0.009	0.097	−0.047	−1162.32	−1.087	−0.033
Computer	0.006	0.079	−0.003	2438.64	2.108	0.056
Educ.	0.214	0.411	−0.039	746.16	2.159	0.089
Engin.	0.051	0.220	0.153	316.68	0.637	0.020
Fine & ap. arts	0.089	0.286	−0.272	−973.55	−2.107	−0.080
For. lang.	0.044	0.207	−0.097	−1128.19	−2.154	−0.067
Health	0.019	0.137	−0.067	−454.83	−0.603	−0.018
Home econ.	0.019	0.137	−0.045	620.30	0.809	0.024
Law	0.022	0.148	0.175	7271.58	10.831	0.313
Letters	0.080	0.271	−0.034	−302.03	−0.717	−0.023
Math.	0.041	0.200	−0.001	−303.86	0.578	−0.017
Phys. sci.	0.089	0.286	0.150	99.00	0.236	0.008
Psych.	0.041	0.200	0.000	718.88	1.350	0.041
Professor	0.333	0.472	0.720	8993.56	11.466	1.233
Assoc. prof.	0.403	0.491	−0.148	5100.53	6.947	0.728
Asst. prof.	0.237	0.426	−0.521	2682.56	3.932	0.331
Publications	6.323	13.240	0.113	8.98	1.218	0.034
Teach. rating	3.077	0.533	−0.126	187.99	1.004	0.029
Univ. senate	0.503	1.054	0.370	324.20	3.260	0.099
El. comm.	0.189	0.670	0.241	−38.82	−0.263	−0.007
Sen. comm.	1.198	1.751	0.216	6.39	0.109	0.003
Pres. comm.	0.637	1.307	0.142	−78.59	−1.037	−0.029
Appt. comm.	0.044	0.346	−0.047	−274.10	−0.995	−0.027

Dependent
Salary   18536.714 3443.010

Intercept 10514.50   Multiple
Correlation
0.90640

rank is in fact due to the outcome variables and therefore reduces their apparent impact. To determine whether this was the case, an analysis of variance was done on the outcome variables (see table 5-4).

The full professors tend to have spent considerably more time in committee activity than is true of other ranks, but one might rationally question whether service on committees justifies either promotion in rank or considerably higher

Table 5-3
Multiple Regression for Equity Study after Adjustments for Faculty at the University of North Dakota
(n = 312)

Variable	Mean	Standard Deviation	Correlation with Salary	Regression Coefficient	Computed t-Value	Beta
Ph.D.	0.657	0.475	0.365	1079.99	4.589	0.149
B.A.	0.012	0.112	−0.148	557.57	0.641	0.018
Prof.	0.006	0.079	0.067	3196.81	2.670	0.074
3-7 years	0.240	0.428	−0.026	158.40	0.526	0.019
8-12 years	0.275	0.447	0.074	221.49	0.676	0.028
13-17 years	0.134	0.341	0.090	442.96	1.141	0.044
19-22 years	0.051	0.220	0.125	906.15	1.784	0.058
Over 22 years	0.080	0.271	0.169	668.25	1.424	0.052
Grad. prog.	0.868	0.338	0.078	−91.01	−0.297	−0.008
Sex	0.855	0.351	0.268	361.03	1.253	0.037
Biol. sc.	0.044	0.207	0.118	−100.49	−0.202	−0.006
Bus. & man.	0.105	0.308	0.061	1808.37	4.941	0.162
Comm.	0.009	0.097	−0.049	−1139.43	−1.106	−0.032
Computer	0.006	0.079	−0.005	2361.01	2.118	0.054
Educ.	0.214	0.411	−0.042	724.52	2.176	0.086
Engin.	0.051	0.220	0.156	401.19	0.838	0.025
Fine & ap. arts	0.089	0.286	−0.273	−964.05	−2.165	−0.080
For. lang.	0.044	0.207	−0.098	−1162.17	−2.303	−0.070
Health	0.019	−0.137	−0.063	−337.29	−0.464	−0.013
Home econ.	0.019	0.137	−0.048	543.25	0.735	0.021
Law	0.022	0.148	0.176	7342.87	11.354	0.317
Letters	0.080	0.271	−0.036	−317.21	−0.782	−0.025
Math.	0.041	0.200	0.001	−235.44	−0.465	−0.013
Phys. sci.	0.089	0.286	0.154	141.75	0.351	0.011
Psych.	0.041	0.200	−0.004	691.00	1.347	0.040
Professor	0.333	0.472	0.723	9050.52	11.979	1.245
Assoc. prof.	0.403	0.491	−0.142	5174.23	7.316	0.740
Asst. prof.	0.237	0.426	−0.530	2698.64	4.106	0.335
Publications	6.323	13.240	0.111	7.89	1.110	0.030
Teach. rating	3.077	0.533	−0.124	219.33	1.216	0.034
Univ. senate	0.503	1.054	0.367	298.29	3.114	0.091
El. comm.	0.189	0.670	0.240	−41.61	−0.292	−0.008
Sen. comm.	1.198	1.751	0.217	2.12	0.037	0.001
Pres. comm.	0.637	1.307	0.149	−61.61	−0.844	−0.023
Appt. comm.	0.044	0.346	−0.049	−286.46	−1.079	−0.028

Dependent
  Salary   18612.140   3431.767

Intercept   10418.76   Multiple
                                        Correlation

                        0.91287

salaries. While professors have a higher mean research output, this difference is offset by two considerations; publication activity is nonnormally distributed (the standard deviation is approximately twice the mean), and the mean output is less than a single article a year. Also the publication activity of faculty at all ranks tended to be almost nonexistent. Previously Martin (1977) was unable to

Table 5-4

Academic Rank and Outcome Variables and Salary Variables

(n = 312)

Variable	Professor *(n = 104)*	Associate Professor *(n = 126)*	Assistant Professor *(n = 74)*	Instructor *(n = 8)*	F
Research	8.99	6.44	3.06	0.13	3.58
Teaching	2.99	3.09	3.15	3.34	2.01
University senate	0.87	0.48	0.09	0	9.08
Elected committees	0.48	0.06	0.01	0	10.88
Senate committees	1.56	1.43	0.42	0.13	8.67
Presidential committees	0.82	0.77	0.22	0.13	4.18
Appointed committees	0.04	0.05	0.03	0.25	1.01
1977-1978 Contracted salary	22037	17918	15321	12521	186.43
1977-1978 Salary (after equity adjustment)	22119	18020	15350	12521	196.90
1977-1978 Salary residual (negative only)[a]	407	682	708	2465	15.62
Salary equity adjustment	82	102	29	0.00	4.11

[a]Only negative residuals were used because these were the identified cases where an adjustment could be made; those who had a positive residual would not have their salary decreased.

discern any plausible explanation for promotion at the University of North Dakota, other than having served in some administrative capacity. Thus the "policy" regarding salaries is both more complex and simpler than is addressed by the regression analysis. It is simpler, in that knowing a person's degree, rank, and participation in a few selected departments can give almost as good an indication of salary as knowing the complete set of information. It is more complex in that the variables that determine rank are not sufficiently known to be of much predictive value.

What then could be said about the adjustment process, in an overall sense? Apparently no major effects on the salary determination machinery have taken place. Even when a deliberate attempt is made to implement a policy at the local level, some noncompliance occurs. For example, in the present case associate professors received higher equity increases than professors even though the intention was the opposite. Implicit in the state board action was that the negative residuals be closely examined in the salary adjustment process; other than as limiters of the possible adjustment, the residuals were not highly related to actual increases. Among just those who had a negative residual ($N = 172$), the correlation between negative residuals and equity increase is 0.06. This disturbing finding could be partially due to the mesh of the several criteria used to address inequity. Probably the politics of the departments and refusal to change "pecking orders" were involved as well. Interestingly, the correlations between the equity increase and the research and teaching variables were respectively −0.05 and 0.06.

Table 5-5 shows an additional dimension to the equity increases. Among

Table 5-5
Equity Increases at the University of North Dakota

	Professors	Associate Professors	Assistant Professors	Instructors
Total number	104	126	74	8
Eligible for equity increase	36	74	54	8
Received an equity increase	24	46	9	0
Range of equity increases	$52-$870	$80-$572	$70-$443	none
Mean increase of those receiving equity increase	$355	$279	$241	none

those eligible for equity increases, professors were more likely to receive them. Faculty at the lower two ranks were almost shut out from equity increases.

Looking at the data yet another way, one can see that twenty-one faculty had twenty or more points on the research scale (two refereed articles by a single author per year); ten of these faculty were eligible for equity increases. Three actually received equity increases ($80 to $120 with a mean of $100). Clearly research played no important part in the equity adjustment process. In a similar vein, seventeen faculty had ratings of 3.8 or above (on a scale where 4.0 is the upper end). Of those, eight were eligible for equity increases and five received increases, from $100 to $300, with a mean of $178. Excellence in teaching, as inferred from the student ratings, was not highly rewarded in the equity process either.

What, then, can be learned from the North Dakota equity study that would be useful to apply (or avoid applying) to other states? First, the term *equity* is one of those ethereal terms that apparently most people think they understand; however, the term means very different things to different people, and it is useful to have an explicit agreement among those who will make decisions regarding equity; better still, all faculty should understand exactly how equity is to be considered and all procedures used for equity adjustments are to be made. The politics of equity adjustments is more difficult to address. Something has gone awry when reasoning gives way to "he who has the most votes in his back pocket." And politics has a way of entering the arena when real money is being used. Arguments will occur on deciding which variables are to be used, whether a regression study or some other process is used. Politics actually has a way of permeating the entire process; monitoring each stage with reporting of information in small public meetings appears useful. One point that is not obvious is the accuracy of information, particularly where that information has been collected at another institution. One major advantage of the regression approach described here is regard for individuals who have large negative residuals. This process would require decision makers to address the issue of individuals who appear underpaid; why are they underpaid? If the answers to this question are not sufficient to convince a reasonable person, then the institution should comply with reasonable compensation.

References

Martin, M. "Promotion Policies Examined by Rank and Sex at the University of North Dakota." *Journal of Teaching and Learning* 3, no. 1 (1977):41-46.

Ward, J.H., and Jennings, E.E. *Introduction to Linear Models.* Englewood Cliffs, N.J.: Prentice-Hall, 1973.

Williams, J.D., and Martin M. "Equalization of Salaries for Higher Education in North Dakota; or, Equal Pay for Equal Work." Paper presented at the Association of Institutional Research, Upper Midwest Meeting, Cedar Falls, Iowa, November 2, 1977.

6

Equal Pay for Equal Qualifications? A Model for Determining Race or Sex Discrimination in Salaries

John A. Muffo,
Larry Braskamp, and
Ira W. Langston IV

This chapter describes the application of multiple regression analysis as one of four steps in a procedure recommended for use in the detection and correction of salary inequities, based on a study done at the University of Illinois at Urbana-Champaign. The Illinois study resulted in identification of potential inequities and a distribution plan that was initially limited to women. Chapter 10, which describes an alternative approach, was developed in part as a reaction to what Birnbaum perceives to be errors in the procedures used in chapter 6.

Discrimination in salary allocation procedures due to race, sex, or other variables unrelated to merit has been getting increased attention recently in higher education. The Equal Pay Act of 1963, the Civil Rights Act of 1964, and Title IX of the Education Amendments Act of 1972 have made salary discrimination due to race or sex illegal. One of the major problems confronted by an institution of higher education, however, is identifying the existence and extent of discrimination, since criteria used in determining salaries are seldom made explicit, particularly on an institutionwide scale. Even if such criteria have been made explicit, there is almost always disagreement as to how well certain individuals have met these criteria.

One approach to solving the salary inequity problem is to ask those responsible for establishing salary policies to review the status of individuals who might be victims of sex or racial discrimination. This relatively subjective mode of operation risks the possibility of requiring people to incriminate themselves, since past discriminatory decisions, if they occurred, were frequently made by some of the same people being asked to review current salaries. Even though important, nonquantifiable factors can be included in such review processes, critics can claim with some justification that the subjective approach will only perpetuate past inequities.

An alternative approach would include the use of a more objective (quantifiable) methodology to determine the existence and extent of salary discrimination. One method would be to match a Caucasian male with a woman or minority person with similar background and ability and then determine whether their salaries are comparable. This procedure, known as counterparting, has been recommended by some (Nevill, 1975), but it is only slightly better than a purely subjective approach. Obviously counterparting presents the initial problem of matching; even in very large departments or institutions, two individuals are seldom exactly alike in ability and experience. A related problem is that possible victims of discrimination are frequently clustered in departments, such as home economics in the case of women, where there are few if any counterparts and certainly none that are similar in merit. Because of the problems surrounding the matching process and the inevitable faculty animosity generated by it, counterparting cannot be recommended as an objective procedure in ferreting out salary inequities.

A second general approach that goes beyond the use of counterparting is the use of multiple regression techniques to predict salaries from merit factors. Faculty must still be matched to a certain extent, but statistical techniques allow for differences in merit factors in predicting salaries. Faculty with different merit factors will have different predicted salaries using multiple regression, so exact matches are unnecessary; yet only explicit, objective variables need be included in the resulting prediction equation. Although fraught with its own set of difficulties, multiple regression appears to be the best objective technique currently available for determining the existence and extent of discrimination.

Recognition of the objective nature of multiple regression as a technique for examining salary inequities has been growing. Scott (1977), in a widely circulated work, contends that the salary equity process is a relatively simple matter of plugging in a few variables, such as time in service and highest degree, and objectively determining salaries. The U.S. Office of Civil Rights seems to hold a similar opinion as expressed in its agreement with the University of Wisconsin, dated December 16, 1977 (*Change,* 1978):

> The University will conduct an analysis to determine potential salary inequities. In one part of the analysis, professional job-related criteria will be identified as basic variables for use in the analysis. Basic variables will be quantified and include: department, rank, time in rank, and measure(s) of length of professional service. Other valid quantifiable variables may be included, provided, however, that prior to inclusion the university shall consult with OCR regarding inclusion of those variables. Using these variables, the University will conduct valid statistical or other empirically verifiable and auditable studies, such as a multiple regression analysis of faculty and academic staff salaries to identify wage discrepancies.
>
> The administration will provide guidelines to administrative units, copies of which will be sent to OCR for its review at the earliest possible date, which will include a description of administratively

approved salary determinants, explicit instructions that every identified inequity must be remedied, detailed explanations of how equity adjustments will be funded, and notification that documentation of the review process must be forwarded to the appropriate dean's or administrative unit head's office and to the chancellor's office. In no case will assertions, verbal or written, unsupported by specific comparative analysis be considered as justification for wage discrepancies. Both reviewing offices will carefully review the findings of the administrative unit's review and return to the unit for further action any cases in which the documentation does not support the review conclusions.

Although statements made by federal officials since the Wisconsin agreement suggest a moderation of the straight formula approach, this agreement does show an inclination toward the use of *only* quantifiable criteria in the salary equity process.

Multiple regression techniques have their own weaknesses. The problems concerning the use of multiple regression involve the nature of the statistical technique itself. For example, multiple regression can be used to predict only a portion of a person's salary, frequently less than 50 percent. In addition, the standard deviations involved are usually quite large. As a result of the latter, using traditional cutoff points such as the 0.05 probability level reveals that few, if any, faculty members are victims of discrimination. Much lower confidence levels yield more victims of discrimination, but these are less acceptable statistically.

Another criticism involves the concept of predicting salaries from merit criteria while not also predicting merit criteria from salaries. Birnbaum (1977) has pointed out that one might appear to be a victim of discrimination when salaries are predicted from merit factors, while no discrimination is apparent when predicting from salaries back to merit factors (see also chapter 10).

These weaknesses inherent in the use of multiple regression do not necessarily preclude their utilization in salary equity decisions, but they do point to the need for something beyond a strict formula approach.

The University of Illinois at Urbana-Champaign Model

A careful review of the literature on multiple regression and salary equity, as well as discussions with other institutional representatives and our own experiences at the University of Illinois at Urbana-Champaign (UIUC), lead to the conclusion that neither a purely subjective approach nor one using multiple regression in a formula manner is the most desirable way of determining salary inequities. For this reason a four-step salary equity review process utilizing both objective (multiple regression) techniques and additional committee evaluations is recommended. Certain aspects of this model have been discussed by Braskamp, Langston, and Muffo (1978) and Braskamp, Muffo, and Langston, (1978).

The UIUC model suggests a four-phase process using different types of judgment at each stage and making different sets of demands on the institution during each of the four phases. The phases are summarized as follows: phase I: policy; phase II: data collection and analysis; phase III: salary adjustment determination; phase IV: follow-up and monitoring.

Phase I: Policy

The policy phase is possibly the most important and least discussed of the four. It is recommended that a campuswide committee of respected faculty and administrators decide several important points before any data are gathered. The most obvious question is who should be included in the analyses—women, various minorities, or both. One suggestion on this point is to first gather data assuming possible discrimination against all women and minorities and then test for group differences using multiple regression. If no group differences are found, assume differences in salary are due to individual rather than group differences, just as they are for majority males. This procedure allows the widest possible coverage of groups, yet it does not require groups showing no discriminatory pattern to be included in the final analysis.

Another policy decision concerns cutoff points. That is, how far below the predicted salary must a faculty member be paid for him or her to be included for further review? These cutoff points can be determined after the regression analysis has yielded predicted salaries, but the decision will probably be more objective and less controversial if made beforehand. Such cutoffs may vary by rank if based on dollar amounts, or they may utilize a percentage limit.

A third, complex policy decision is which variables to include in the multiple regression analysis. Most agree that variables such as highest degree and length of service should be included, but beyond these two compromise might be necessary. Depending on the mission of the institution, other variables considered for use might include rank appointment status (nine- or eleven-month), years of professional experience, publications, grant dollars, teaching awards and evaluations, peer evaluations, some measure of the "market" in that discipline (such as veterinarians versus humanists), and so on. The problem is that some of these variables are not acceptable to all individuals and institutions as fair predictors of salary. In addition, a case can be made that certain variables such as rank are themselves affected by discrimination, so using such variables to predict salaries is simultaneously redundant and discriminatory. The more variables excluded before data gathering, however, the lower the correlation and consequently the lower the predictability of the resulting prediction equation. Obviously trade-offs are necessary.

One suggested approach is to include as many variables as might be acceptable, then determine by stepwise multiple regression which ones contribute significantly to the prediction equation. Only those adding significantly to the prediction equation need be included in analyzing salaries. If a seemingly important variable such as teaching awards is not included in the final prediction equation, however, faculty acceptance might be hindered, even if that variable is not statistically significant. The point is important, for by the nature of multiple regression, the salaries of different people will fall beyond the cutoff points, depending on what variables are included in the prediction equation.

Phase II: Data Collection and Analysis

The data collection and analysis stage is the most mechanical of the four phases once policies have been established. Majority males are matched by department with women and minorities, then included in the data-gathering process. Data on all included faculty are collected from existing sources and by use of questionnaires. The data for the majority males are used to build a prediction equation that fits them. The data for the matched women and/or minorities are then substituted in the majority male prediction equation and salaries are predicted for each faculty member. Those whose salaries fall below their predicted salaries by amounts larger than the cutoffs are "flagged" for further review. Those whose actual salaries are within the cutoff range are eliminated from immediate further consideration.

Some statistical techniques can be used during this phase to increase predictability. One way of doing this is to divide the majority males into match groups, for example, all men matched to women as one subgroup. Since these subgroups tend to include fewer departments in most cases, departmental differences are reduced and a better prediction equation can be built. Another advantage is that women and minorities can be measured against their respective matched majority males rather than all the majority males as a group; in other words, the matching of individuals is more appropriate.

Besides matching subgroups, one can attempt to improve prediction by making some of the variables nonlinear. Publications, for example, frequently have a declining value, with the first few being most important, so the logarithm of the number of journal articles might yield a higher correlation than the number itself. Trial and error of such nonlinear variables may yield a prediction equation with both linear and nonlinear variables, depending on which combination yields the most predictability, all within the confines of policies established in phase I.

Phase III: Salary Adjustment and Determination

During the third phase of the salary equity review process, individuals flagged for further review are given the option of review by committees (departmental, college, or university) for possible salary adjustments. Some people, for personal reasons, will refuse the review. Others not flagged may feel cheated, so all members of the group being investigated (women and/or minorities) should have the option for further review. Our experience has been that only a few of the people not flagged opt for further review, for whatever reason. We also suspect that some who refuse reviews have been promised adjustments if they do not go through the committee structure, thus keeping the matter in the department. Some may also be influenced to keep silent by more negative factors.

The unit review committees in phase III must have some guidelines to follow, including sources and amounts of funds available for salary adjustments. They should also be well informed about the procedures and variables used for flagging. They are then free to include other, nonquantifiable evidence submitted by those being reviewed in deciding what adjustments should be made. After careful review and documentation of reasons for their actions, the committee members then forward their final recommendations to the proper administrator for action.

Phase IV: Follow-up and Monitoring

The final phase of the salary equity review process is the follow-up and monitoring phase. This is the stage at which committee actions are reviewed for possible discriminatory practices. In addition, salary adjustments may be given by committees without the support of the usual decision makers resulting, for instance, in an equity increase but no normal departmental increase in the same year. Using the equity increase to replace a normal increment would frequently leave the person reviewed further behind in salary than before the review, clearly an unacceptable result. In short, then, phase IV suggests a systematic monitoring of salaries in the years following the initial salary equity review. It might even be deemed necessary to repeat the whole process a year or two after the initial study. This monitoring process, when used together with the more traditional affirmative action programs of hiring, retention, and promotion can also serve as a constant reminder of the desired goals.

Epilogue

This salary equity process is recommended for cases involving possible sex or race discrimination. The review of individual majority males is dismissed in that no group discrimination is evident with them. This procedure leaves open the question whether only groups or all individuals should be reviewed, that is, whether it is fair and legal to look only at group and not individual differences in salary policies. The term *reverse discrimination* may be used to criticize the approach recommended here.

The legal aspects are complicated and certainly beyond the scope of this chapter. However, *University of Nebraska* v. *Dawes* (1975) appears to provide a legal basis for saying that any strictly formulaic approach must be applied to all individuals. More legal clarification of this issue may be expected to be forthcoming in the near future.

References

Birnbaum, Michael H. "Procedures for the Analysis and Correction of Salary Inequities." Unpublished manuscript, University of Illinois at Urbana-Champaign, 1977.

Braskamp, Larry A., Muffo, John A., and Langston, Ira W. "Determining Salary Equity: Policies, Procedures, and Problems." *Journal of Higher Education* 49 (1978):231-246.

Braskamp, Larry A., Langston, Ira W., and Muffo, John A. "The Usefulness of a Model for Determining Salary Equity." Paper presented at the American Educational Research Association Annual Meeting in Toronto, Canada, March 1978.

"Does the punishment fit the crime?" *Change* 10 (1978):45.

Nevill, D.D. "Achieving Salary Equity." *Educational Record* 56 (1975):266-270.

Scott, Elizabeth L. *Higher Education Salary Evaluation Kit.* Washington, D.C.: American Association of University Professors, 1977.

University of Nebraska v. *Neil Dawes.* U.S. Court of Appeals, Eighth Circuit, 75-1126, 1975.

A Salary Equity Bibliography

Adams, J.S. "Inequity in Social Exchange." In *Advances in Experimental Psychology,* Vol. 2, ed. L. Berkowitz. New York: Academic Press, 1975.

Anderson, N.H. "Equity Judgments as Information Integration." *Journal of Personality and Social Psychology* 33 (1976):291-299.

Bayer, A.E., and Astin, H.S. "Sex Differentials in the Academic Reward System." *Science* 188 (1975):796-802.

Bergmann, B.R., and Maxfield, M., Jr. "How to Analyze the Fairness of Faculty Women's Salaries on Your Own Campus." *AAUP Bulletin* 61 (1975):262-265.

Birnbaum, M.H. "The Nonadditivity of Personality Impressions. *Journal of Experimental Psychology* 102 (1974):537-539.

Birnbaum, M.H. "Reply to the Devil's Advocates: Don't Confound Model Testing and Measurement." *Psychological Bulletin* 81 (1974):854-859.

Birnbaum, M.H. "Procedures for the Analysis and Correction of Salary Inequities." Unpublished manuscript, University of Illinois at Urbana-Champaign, 1977.

Blackburn, R.T., and Clark, M.J. "An Assessment of Faculty Performance: Some Correlates between Administrator, Colleague, Student, and Self Ratings." *Sociology of Education* 48 (1975):242-256.

Braskamp, L.A., and Johnson, D.R. "The Use of a Parity-Equity Model to Evaluate Faculty Salary Policies." *Research in Higher Education* 8 (1978):57-66.

Braskamp, L.A., Langston, I.W., and Muffo, J.A. "The Usefulness of a Model for Determining Salary Equity." Paper presented at the annual meeting of the American Educational Research Association, Toronto, Canada, March 1978.

Braskamp, L.A., Muffo, J.A., and Langston, I.W. Determining Salary Equity: Policies, Procedures, and Problems." *Journal of Higher Education* 49 (1978):231-246.

Brewer, M.B., Campbell, D.T., and Crano, W.D. "Testing a Single-Factor Model as an Alternative to the Misuse of Partial Correlations in Hypothesis-Testing Research." *Sociometry* 33 (1970):1-11.

Brittingham, B.E., et al. "Inequity and Inequality in Salaries: A Case Study in Methodology." Paper presented at the Association for Institutional Research Annual Forum, Los Angeles, May 1976.

Buzan, B.C., and Hunt, L.Y. "Evaluating Faculty Performance under the Equal Pay for Equal Work doctrine." *Research in Higher Education* 4 (1976):113-123.

Centra, J.A. "The How and Why of Evaluating Teaching." In *Reviewing and Evaluating Teaching,* ed. J.A. Centra. San Francisco: Josey-Bass, 1977.

"Does the Punishment Fit the Crime?" *Change* 10 (1978):45.

Clark, M.J., Hartnett, R.T., and Baird, L.L. *Assessing Dimensions of Quality in Doctoral Education.* Princeton, N.J.: Educational Testing Service, 1976.

Costin, F., Greenough, W.T., and Menges, R.J. "Student Ratings of College Teaching: Reliability, Validity, Usefulness." *Review of Educational Research* 41 (1971):511-535.

Cox, M., and Astin, A.W. Sex Differentials in Faculty Salaries. *Research in Higher Education* 7 (1977):289-298.

Darlington, R.B. "Another Look at Cultural Fairness." *Journal of Educational Measurement* 8 (1971):71-82.

Dawes, R.M. "Shallow Psychology." *Cognition and Social Behavior,* eds. J.S. Carroll and J.W. Payne. Hillsdale, N.J.: Erlbaum, 1976.

Ferber, M.A., and Loeb, J.A. "Rank, Pay, and Representation of Women on the Faculty at the Urbana-Champaign Campus at the University of Illinois: A Reappraisal." Unpublished manuscript, University of Illinois at Urbana-Champaign, 1977.

Ferber, M.A., and Kordick, B. "Men and Women Ph.D.'s in the Sixties and Seventies." *Industrial and Labor Relations Review* 31, no. 2, pp. 227-238.

Garfield, E. "Citation Analysis as a Tool in Journal Education." *Science* 178 (1972):471-479.

Gordon, N., Morton, T.E., and Braden, I.C. "Faculty Salaries: Is There Discrimination by Sex, Race, and Discipline?" *American Economic Review* 64 (1976):419-447.

Harris, R.J. "Handling Negative Inputs: On the Plausible Equity Formulae." *Journal of Experimental Social Psychology* 12 (1976):194-209.

Jauch, L.R., and Glueck, W.F. "Evaluation of University Professors' Research Performance." *Management Science* 22 (1975):66-75.

Johnson, G.E., and Stafford, F.P. "The Earning and Promotion of Women Faculty." *American Economic Review* 64 (1974):888-903.

Katz, D.A. "The Determinants of Faculty Salaries and Rates of Promotion at a Large University." Doctoral dissertation, University of Illinois at Urbana-Champaign, 1971.

Katz, D.A. "Faculty Salaries, Promotions, and Productivity at a Large University." *American Economic Review* 63 (1973):469-477.

Koch, J.V., and Chizmar, J.F. *The Economics of Affirmative Action.* Lexington, Mass.: Lexington Books, D.C. Heath and Company, 1976.

Loeb J.A., Ferber, M.A., and Lowry, H.M. "The Effectiveness of Affirmative Action for Women." *Journal of Higher Education* 49 (1978):218-230.

Lord, F.M. "A Paradox in the Interpretation of Group Comparisons." *Psychological Bulletin* 68 (1967):304-305.

Malkiel, B.G., and Malkiel, J.A. "Male-Female Pay Differentials in Professional Employment." *American Economic Review* 63 (1973):693-705.

Miller, G.A. *Psychology: The Science of Mental Life.* New York: Harper and Row, 1962, pp. 129-146.

Nevill, D.D. "Achieving Salary Equity." *Educational Record* 56 (1975):266-270.

Porter, A.L., and Wolfe, D. "Utility of the Doctoral Dissertation." *American Psychologist* 30 (1975):1054-1061.

Reagan, B.B., and Maynard, B.J. "Sex Discrimination in Universities: An Approach through Internal Market Analysis." *AAUP Bulletin* 60 (1974):13-21.

Scott, E.L. *Higher Education Salary Evaluation Kit.* Washington, D.C.: American Association of University of Professors, 1977.

Smith, R., and Fiedler, F.E. "The Measurement of Scholarly Work: A Critical Review of the Literature." *Educational Record* 52 (1971):225-232.

Smock, H.R., and Crooks, T. "A Plan for the Comprehensive Evaluation of College Teaching." *Journal of Higher Education* 47 (1976):51-64.

University of Nebraska v. *Neil Dawes.* U.S. Court of Appeals, Eighth Circuit, 75-1126, 1975.

Walster, E., Berscheid, E., and Walster, G.W. "New Directions in Equity Research." *Journal of Personality and Social Psychology* 25 (1973):151-176.

Walster, G.W. "The Walster et al. (1973) Equity Formula: A Correction." *Representative Research in Social Psychology* 6 (1975):63-64.

7

A Method for Monitoring University Faculty Salary Policies for Sex Bias

Larry O. Hunter

This chapter represents the application of a regression model to a small state university. It differs from most other models by including administrative position as one of the independent variables. Most other studies see administrative appointments as possibly confounded with unfair independent variables. This study accounted for all variation in salary before sex was considered.

During the past few years many studies have reported on the use of multiple linear regression in the analysis of faculty salary differentials. This study used data on all full-time academic faculty at a state university, a relatively small land grant institution. A model was developed using rank, time in current rank, highest degree, administrative position, and academic department as independent variables and was used to investigate the effect of sex as an additional independent variable. Over 85 percent of the variation in salaries across faculty members is explained by the model. The partial correlation with sex was found to be zero when controlled for the other independent variables. Since many departments had no women faculty members and at least one had no men faculty members, the departmental regression weights were compared with average salaries by rank for the same academic disciplines obtained from a nationwide salary study. These comparisons resulted in correlation coefficients of 0.75, 0.88, and 0.84 with average salaries for professors, associate professors, and assistant professors respectively.

Background

At the university studied there is no formal salary schedule, and salaries are set by individual contract. Salary increases are usually awarded on three or more bases such as across-the-board, merit, and other adjustments. Initial salaries are set by negotiation, and until recently no formal model such as the one used in this analysis was available for estimating an appropriate salary range for a particular set of credentials. Just three years earlier over $100,000 in back pay and special adjustments was awarded to women faculty members. However, a review of average salaries such as those in table 7-1 raised the question whether inequity between salaries for men and women still existed.

An increasing number of authors recommend the use of multiple linear regression in faculty salary policy analysis. Malkiel and Malkiel (1973, pp. 699-700) state the following:

> Gross differences in average salaries between men and women do not indicate the presence of discrimination. If women, on average, have less education and job experience than men, we should anticipate that their average salaries would be lower. Discrimination can be said to exist only if women with the same characteristics as men tend to receive lower salaries.

Many of these studies have dealt with sex discrimination in salary setting. They include studies on single institutions, studies on large numbers of institutions, and even international comparisons such as that of Blackstone and Fulton (1975). Most of them have reported a significant negative correlation between salary and being a woman faculty member even when controlling for all the other independent variables that are significantly related to salary in their data. Many of them, for example, Bayer and Astin (1968), Astin and Bayer (1972), and Scott (1977) conclude that such findings are conservative estimates of existing sex discrimination because some of the independent variable values such as rank are set by a process that may allow sex discrimination to be practiced in setting these values.

Development of the Model

Some previous analysis using multiple linear regression techniques had been done at the university being studied. Both 1975-76 faculty salaries and 1976-77

Table 7-1
1966-77 Average Salaries for Full-Time Faculty Members by Sex and Rank

Rank		Men	Women	Total
Professors	n	185	10	195
	$\bar{x}$	20,838	19,500	20,769
Associate professors	n	155	13	168
	$\bar{x}$	16,451	16,049	16,420
Assistant professors	n	103	27	130
	$\bar{x}$	14,153	13,084	13,931
Instructors	n	14	11	25
	$\bar{x}$	11,625	11,157	11,419
All ranks	n	457	61	518
	$\bar{x}$	17,561	14,420	17,191

faculty salaries had been analyzed with a model using rank, years in current rank, highest degree, administrative responsibility, and academic college as independent variables. Statistics from this model for 1976-77 are shown in table 7-2 as the college model. Results from a more abbreviated model, ignoring academic field altogether, confirmed that a significant portion of the differences in men and women's salaries indicated in table 7-1 could be attributed to differences between salary levels in the academic colleges.

At about this time a state commission on human rights in the same state as the university being studied took an official position that differences in salary levels between academic specialties did not violate equal pay for equal work regulations if maintaining such a difference was a common, industrywide practice. In the case of the university this could mean that salary differences between academic fields should be approximately the same as at similar universities across the country that employ faculty in the same field. The model was altered by replacing the college variable (the university had eight colleges) with a department variable (the university had forty departments). The results of this analysis are also shown in table 7-2. Essentially all the variation in salaries related to sex can be attributed to other independent variables in this simple model.

Evaluation of the Department Differentials

The university had been a regular participant in an annual faculty salary survey conducted by the Office of Institutional Research at Oklahoma State University. This survey collected and presented information on faculty salaries by academic discipline (department) and by academic rank. Most of the land grant institutions in the country were participants.

Table 7-2
Result of Multiple Linear Regression on Several Models
Based on Rank, Years in Rank, Highest Degree, and
Administrative Title

Model	R^2	S.D.	B Value for Men
No field model	0.72	2617	516
College model	0.83	1547	237
Department model including sex variable	0.86	1424	32
Department model without sex variable	0.86	1423	20[a]

[a]B value calculated using residuals from the department model without sex variable as the dependent variable and sex as the only independent variable.

The average salaries from this study (Office of Institutional Research, Oklahoma State University, 1977) for the forty disciplines most closely related to the university's forty departments were compared to the department weights from the model. Comparisons were made for average salaries from each of the ranks professor, associate professor, and assistant professor. The correlation coefficients from these comparisons were 0.75 with average salaries for the professor rank, 0.88 with average salaries at the associate professor rank, and 0.84 with average salaries at the assistant professor rank. Figure 7-1 shows the distribution of the regression weights for university departments plotted against salaries for associate professors from the survey.

The university does not operate schools of medicine or veterinary medicine, and a large number of the academic fields are bunched toward the lower end of the ranges for average salaries and for regression weights. Those on the upper ranges represent fields in engineering, business, and law. Those at the lower end include fields in arts and sciences, education, and agriculture and natural resources.

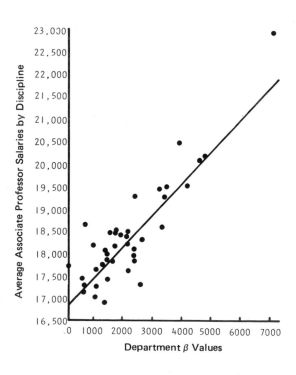

Figure 7-1. β Values for the University Departments Plotted against Average Salaries from the 1976-77 OSU Salary Survey for Associate Professors from Similar Disciplines

Summary

This analysis demonstrates that while women faculty at the university studied are paid lower salaries than men faculty, essentially all these differences can be accounted for by the regression model developed. The most important factors are the small number of women represented in the higher-paying ranks and higher-paying academic disciplines. The university's treatment of salary differentials between academic disciplines closely follows practices at a large number of similar institutions.

The question whether there is sex discrimination in the university's promotion and rank-setting practices has not been addressed in this study but is being addressed separately in a broader context than salary implications alone. The only conclusion here is that if it is determined that there are problems in promotion and rank-setting, then any corrections or adjustments in academic rank would have to be accompanied by the appropriate adjustments in salary in order to maintain the balance described by the model used in this study.

References

Astin, H.S., and Bayer, A.E. "Sex Discrimination in Academe." *Educational Record* 53 (1972):101-118.

Bayer, A.E., and Astin, H.S. "Sex Difference in Academic Rank and Salary among Science Doctorates in Teaching." *Journal of Human Resources* 16 (1968):192-193.

Bayer, A.E. "Sex Differentials in the Academic Reward System." *Science* 188 (1975):796-802.

Beaumont, M.S. "Efficiency and Equity: The Single Salary Schedule in Public Higher Education." *AAUP Bulletin* 64 (1978):19-25.

Blackstone, T., and Fulton, O. "Sex Discrimination among University Teachers: A British-American Comparison." *British Journal of Sociology* 26 (1975):261-275.

Gordon, N., Morton, T., and Braden, I. "Faculty Salaries: Is There Discrimination by Sex, Race, and Discipline?" *American Economic Review* 64 (1974):419-427.

Harris, A.S. "The Second Sex in Academe." *AAUP Bulletin* 56 (1970):283-295.

Johnson, G.E., and Stafford, F.P. "The Earnings and Promotion of Women Faculty." *American Economic Review* 64 (1974):888-903.

Malkiel, B. and Malkiel, J. "Male-Female Pay Differentials in Professional Employment." *American Economic Review* 63 (1973):693-705.

McLaughlin, G.W., Smart, J.C., and Montgomery, J.R. "Factors Which Comprise Salary." Paper presented at the Association for Institutional Research Forum, May 1977.

Nevill, D.D. "Achieving Salary Equity." *Educational Record* 56 (1975):266-270.
Office of Institutional Research, Oklahoma State University 1976-1977 "Faculty Salary Survey by Discipline," vol. 1, 1977.
Scott, E.L. "Higher Education Salary Evaluation Kit." Washington, D.C.: American Association of University Professors, 1977.

8

Salary Inequities and Differences: One College's Attempt at Identification and Adjustment

Robert E. Wall

This chapter describes the detection procedures at Towson State College with a faculty of approximately five hundred. Only three variables—rank, years of experience, and degree held—produced a multiple R of 0.92. The author describes adjustment procedures used and the political and practical ramifications of the attempt to distribute inequity adjustments and concludes with some practical advice for conducting such an analysis and adjustment.

Recent events indicate an increased concern with economic discrimination in higher education. This report describes how a moderately large (approximately five-hundred faculty members) suburban-urban master's degree-granting institution responded to external and internal concerns about salary differences perceived as inequities. This chapter describes that institution's attempt to develop a method for identifying and ameliorating faculty salary differences or inequities. One major assumption was that the method was to be acceptable to the faculty as well as to the administration and still work within the constraints of a tight budget.

Perspective

Until enactment of recent public policy measures such as affirmative action, the Equal Pay Act, and Title IX of the Higher Education Act of 1972, designed to eliminate salary inequities, little systematic exploration had been made of the factors leading to salary differentials among faculty members. Several large-scale studies (Johnson and Stafford, 1974; Gordon, Morton, and Braden, 1974; Katz, 1973) investigated large samples of faculty members to ascertain the magnitude and possible causes of observed salary differences. Although such studies discovered salary differences that could be related to membership in various identifiable groups (sex, race), there was never complete agreement about the causes of observed salary differences and, more important, whether observed differences are inequities. Some salary differences are based on bona fide seniority or merit considerations. (Obviously there is ample room for disagreement about what constitutes legitimate seniority or merit differentials.)

Detection Procedures

A number of methods have been proposed for determining salary inequities. They range from the plan that all holding the same rank should receive the same salary, to defining as inequities those whose salary is below the mean for that rank, to regression models either within ranks or within an entire institution. Towson State University chose a linear regression model to determine the relationship between observed salary and a set of independent variables: data first employed at the institution, sex, race, academic department, and total years of professional experience.

The original stepwise regression model used all the independent variables. Three variables—rank, years of experience, and degrees held—provided a multiple R of 0.92. This is fortunate for the institution, because there is less controversy concerning the appropriateness of these variables for investigating salary differences than there is for the remaining variables. The decision was then made to use these three variables as the basis for determining salary inequities.

The revised model was used to estimate each individual's predicted salary. Individuals earning less than their predicted salary were identified as examples of possible salary inequity. Since the true relationship between salary and the independent variables may be more complex than the model can accommodate, several two- and three-way cross tabulations were developed to detect possible nonlinear effects.

Adjustment Procedures

Approximately $88,000 was to be available to adjust the identified inequities. These adjustments were to be made after normal promotions and salary raises had been determined.

The following explanation was sent to the faculty by the academic dean:

> The new method mathematically determines the relationship (correlation) between the salary and the three factors of rank, total years of experience, and degree. It analyzes the entire salary structure for the whole faculty; it assumes that as faculty have been promoted, gained years of experience and earned higher degrees, they have earned more than those who have not. It does not make a value judgment about this structure but rather determines the influence that each of the factors has had in determining what a faculty member earns . . . . Using this method, it is possible to project a faculty member's salary based on his/her rank, years of experience and degree (Shaw, 1975).

Four constraints were placed on the determination of salary adjustments.

1. A salary could not be adjusted above the ceiling for that rank.
2. All individuals at the two highest ranks, as well as individuals in disciplines where the master's degree is considered the terminal degree, were to be treated as holders of the Ph.D.
3. Only full-time faculty members were included in the study.
4. Only individuals identified as underpaid were to have their salaries adjusted.

Results

Although no discernible pattern of sex- or race-related salary inequities was noted, this model did identify disproportionately more individuals of certain ranks and/or departments as inequity cases. Approximately two hundred of the five hundred faculty members were identified for inequity salary adjustments. The total amount required by the regression model to complete adjustments was approximately $250,000. Inasmuch as less than $90,000 was available, actual adjustments were made at the rate of 34 percent of the indicated adjustment. The regression equation employed is described in table 8-1. The interrelationships among the dependent and independent variables are presented in table 8-2.

The regression model employed did not use sex or ethnic group as independent variables. It was assumed that if such discrimination had been practiced, the number of and amounts of the adjustment to the various classifications of faculty members would reflect this discrimination. To investigate the pattern of adjustments to various ethnic groups, the data in table 8-3

Table 8-1
Results of Regression Analysis

	Mult R	B
Rank	0.872	2293.93
Years of experience	0.921	219.05
Degree held	0.923	481.37
Constant	7582.44	
Standard error	1626.52	

Table 8-2
Intercorrelation Matrix of Dependent and Independent Variables

	Rank	Years of Experience	Degree Held
Salary	0.82	0.78	0.50
Rank		0.57	0.55
Years of experience			0.18

Table 8-3
Summary of Adjustments Classified by Recipients' Reported Race

Race	Mean	Standard Deviation	Number of Adjustments	Percentage
Black (n = 18)	359.80	183.76	5	28
Oriental (n = 11)	527.40	292.40	5	45
Spanish surname (n = 2)	299.00	0.00	1	50
Other (n = 412)	432.82	307.12	203	49
Total: 443			214	48

were compiled. No further analysis was attempted because of the small numbers in the ethnic classifications.

Tables 8-4 and 8-5 are concerned with the salary adjustments made to various groups of faculty members classified according to sex and rank or academic division. Although the overall proportions of male and female faculty members receiving adjustments were similar (46 percent versus 52 percent) and the mean adjustment values were close ($432.25 versus $433.44), there are wide discrepancies within rank and among academic disciplines.

Some Procedural Considerations

The completion of a study such as this revolves around two basic problems. The first is getting agreement about the appropriate variables to be considered in

Table 8-4
Summary of Adjustments Classified by Recipients' Rank and Sex

		Mean	Standard Deviation	Number	Adjustments (%)
Instructor	(n = 50)	255.00	129.30	6	12
Male	(n = 29)	221.50	28.99	2	
Female	(n = 21)	271.75	162.70	4	
Assistant professor	(n = 156)	307.08	221.55	89	57
Male	(n = 84)	242.67	174.68	46	
Female	(n = 72)	375.98	246.46	43	
Associate professor	(n = 133)	530.24	308.10	82	62
Male	(n = 92)	510.32	272.11	56	
Female	(n = 41)	573.15	426.13	26	
Full professor	(n = 104)	547.54	362.20	37	36
Male	(n = 80)	602.61	394.10	28	
Female	(n = 24)	376.22	150.09	9	
Total	433	432.71	303.42	214	
Male	285	432.25	309.34		
Female	158	433.44	317.16		

Table 8-5
Summary of Adjustments Classified by Recipients' Sex and Division

Division		Mean	Standard Deviation	Number of Adjustments	Percentage of Group
Social science, humanities					
Male	(n = 79)	502.08	309.34	38	48
Female	(n = 27)	498.00	242.84	17	63
Fine arts					
Male	(n = 66)	458.97	302.97	35	53
Female	(n = 30)	468.39	403.08	18	60
Natural science					
Male	(n = 77)	301.31	192.46	39	51
Female	(n = 27)	412.71	310.35	17	63
Education					
Male	(n = 37)	671.76	387.63	13	35
Female	(n = 36)	497.13	360.57	16	44
Applied science					
Male	(n = 26)	236.13	173.99	8	31
Female	(n = 38)	282.69	296.51	13	34
Total (n = 443)					
Male	(n = 285)	432.25	309.34	132	46
Female	(n = 158)	433.44	317.16	82	52
				214	48

determining the salary differentials. There are many problems in deciding which variables are important. These variables will have to be chosen with each campus in mind. If publication, rate of publication, and quality of publication are important considerations, one must still decide whether there is a reasonably objective way to gather the information. If community service and academic committee work are to be considered, then the relative weight that each of these variables should contribute must be determined.

Rank is often chosen as a variable because different standards within departments, divisions, and colleges are widely held to be important in determining promotion. Often the available information on faculty members does not include quantified details of community service, teaching ability, student ratings, peer ratings, or research and publication; and rank is often used to reflect these differences in academic endeavors. One should be aware of the common concern for the potential systematic bias in determining who is promoted and how early. Related problems included such mundane matters as determining whether a master of fine arts (M.F.A.) is as important in the arts as a Ph.D. is in certain other disciplines. In this study an M.F.A. that represented a terminal degree in the faculty member's discipline was treated the same way as a Ph.D. in disciplines where the Ph.D. is the terminal degree. Another arbitrary decision was to consider all individuals with a full professor rank as having the equivalent of a Ph.D. degree. In another setting these assumptions could easily fail to hold.

The second basic problem of conducting a study such as this has to do with mechanics. It is important to be able to develop the mechanism for gathering the data, quantifying it, and putting it into a format suitable for analysis. If one has survived these first few steps, then the analysis, methods, and data presentation must be determined.

There remains the minor problem of selling the idea to the rest of the faculty, the administration, and other outside agencies that might become involved—labor departments, labor unions, and so forth.

A major problem in dealing with many faculty groups was the lack of understanding of regression analysis. This lack of understanding was evident when many assumed that two hundred of over four hundred salary *differences* in predicted and actual salary were salary discrimination. Many faculty do not realize that multiple regression balances overpredictions and underpredictions. A related problem is the frequent lack of any quantitative understanding in certain audiences. A fascinating example stems from the fact that the average salary for a specific rank or category increases when any individual's salary increases. This upward movement of the mean salary for that faculty group means that individuals given adjustments to bring them up to the current mean will be below the new mean.

Our experience indicates that several approaches to these problems can be taken. Depending on the audience's proclivity for numbers and understanding of the regression approach, one will find varying degrees of support among faculty and administrators. An administrator suggested that all individuals identified as underpaid by the multiple regression equation should have their salaries raised to the predicted level and all individuals identified as overpaid should have their salaries reduced to the predicted levels. Thus one would have a perfect fit between predictors and criterion in a short time. The faculty response to this was predictably unenthusiastic.

A demonstration of the power of multiple regression that is convincing even to the layman appears in chapter 2. For more detail on model building in multiple regression and some procedural pitfalls to avoid, see chapter 4.

Conclusion

Salary differences and inequities now exist on nearly all campuses of higher education. This chapter demonstrates how one moderately sized master's degree—granting institution economically and objectively carried out a salary differential study that used procedures and techniques available to most institutions of higher education.

Epilogue

This procedure for identifying and adjusting salary inequities has been through several iterations at Towson State University. In the last five years over two hundred faculty members have been given equity adjustments totaling several hundred thousand dollars. This procedure has been well accepted by the faculty and administration; each year they have had the opportunity to reject the plan and did not. The faculty have accepted this procedure even though the money made available for equity adjustments has come from money set aside for salary increments. In other words, the faculty have agreed to smaller across-the-board increments to make money available for equity adjustments.

The experience of the last five years has provided the basis for the following observations.

1. There must be faculty participation and administrative cooperation from the start.
2. Everyone involved must recognize that this procedure should be a continuous process, since every promotion, retirement, and addition of new personnel affects the overall salary structure.
3. The adoption of this method reduces the pressure on the administration to justify the allocation of salary monies.
4. There has been a reduction in the feeling among faculty members that salaries are determined by some arbitrary process.
5. There has been increased communication and understanding between the faculty and administration concerning salaries and appropriate resource allocation.
6. The starting salaries of new personnel should be set by the regression values generated. Failure to do so will result in additional inequities in the salary structure.
7. Although this method may seem like a rational approach to analyzing salaries, many value decisions must be made—variables to be included, dollar allocation, eligibility.
8. Not everyone will be happy with this or any other plan.

References

"The Association Receives Exxon Grant." *Academe,* April 1975, p. 3.

Gordon, N.M., Morton, T.M., and Braden, I.C. "Faculty Salaries: Is There Discrimination by Sex, Race, and Discipline?" *American Economic Review* 64 (June 1974):419-427.

Johnson, G.E., and Stafford, F.P. "The Earnings and Promotion of Women." *American Economic Review* 64 (December 1974):888-903.

Katz, D.A. "Faculty Salaries, Promotions, and Productivity in a Large University." *American Economic Review* 63 (June 1973):469-477.

Madden, J.F. *The Economics of Sex Discrimination.* Lexington, Mass.: Lexington Books, D.C. Heath and Co., 1973.

Nie, N.H. *SPSS, Statistical Package for the Social Sciences,* 2nd ed., New York: McGraw-Hill, 1975.

Shaw, K.A., Letter to Faculty. "1974-75 Salary Inequity Study," April 21, 1975.

Taubman, P., and Wales, T. *Higher Education and Earnings: College As an Investment and Screening Device.* New York: McGraw-Hill, 1974.

9

A Multiple Regression Model for Predicting Men's and Women's Salaries in Higher Education

Barbara E. Brittingham,
Thomas R. Pezzullo,
Glenworth A. Ramsay,
John V. Long, and
Roy M. Ageloff

This chapter describes the analyses used at the University of Rhode Island, including specific inquiries with a random sample of faculty on whom measures of scholarly productivity were developed and compared to the discrepancies between their actual and predicted salaries. Policy recommendations designed to foster equity adjustments in the complex setting of higher education conclude the chapter. The specifics of the multiple regression model and its use in other settings are described in chapter 4; one further examination of the material gathered in interviews of a random sample of faculty is found in chapter 11.

In 1976 a study of salaries of faculty at the University of Rhode Island was undertaken to determine whether there were systematic and discriminatory inequities between men's and women's salaries. The population studied was the 694 full-time tenure-track faculty employed by the University of Rhode Island (URI) during the 1975-76 academic year.

The study resulted from a charge to the Affirmative Action Office by the URI president to develop a plan to insure that men and women are paid equally for equal work. The charge was inspired in part by descriptive data available at that time indicating that the average male faculty member was paid more than the average female faculty member at all ranks.

The analyses developed were designed to address the question: To what extent do academic-year salaries systematically differ for men and women at the University of Rhode Island in ways that might be considered discriminatory on the basis of sex? A major assumption of the research team was that differences (inequalities) are not inherently inequities. Certain systematic differences occur in a complex salary system that acknowledge differences in employees with respect to educational level, training, experience, discipline (market conditions),

The authors wish to acknowledge the assistance of Andrea Panciera in the preparation and conduct of this study.

and merit. The principal purpose of the study was to examine the differences remaining after these equitable differences had been accounted for.

This chapter discusses the development of a model, legitimate determiners of salary, the particular model used, and results of the regression analysis. The chapter also presents some indications of the future at URI and a study of the relationship of scholarly productivity to salary for men and women. Finally, the policy and procedural recommendations for establishing salary equity at URI are set forth and explained.

Developing the Model

In data sets that include a large number of variables, descriptive statistics offer a wealth of information but are inefficient at synthesizing relationships among the variables. The descriptive analyses of faculty salaries fail to examine the issue of whether men are paid more than women when rank, degrees, prior experience, and field of study have been systematically taken into account. To address such issues requires inferential statistics.

The use of inferential statistics involves the construction of a model that reflects certain assumptions about the organization of the data and the relationships among the variables. Inferential statistics are then used to test the model to see whether it is an accurate and efficient explanation of the variables in question. In this study the model is a mathematical equation of salary determination; the underlying assumption is that, on the average, salaries are determined by this equation. A mathematical model does not assume that such an equation is explicitly used by those determining salary but rather that their behavior can be represented by such an equation.

The variables that are factors in salary determination and their precise mathematical form is determined by the model builder. The coefficients, that is, the importance and relative impact of the variables, may then be estimated using multiple regression. Standard statistical tests determine whether the results are significant, that is, whether the model is a plausible explanation of reality or merely due to chance.

In determining a suitable model to use, the researchers may select any variables that are quantifiable and decide whether and how to include them in the equation. Variables that cannot be satisfactorily quantified in the population of interest cannot be included. Thus scholarly productivity was not included in the regression analyses, though other studies indicate that it is a significant determinant of salaries, because there was no easily available index of scholarly activity for each member of the URI faculty. (The relationship of scholarly productivity to salary analyses is described later in this chapter.)

An additional step in building the model is deciding which of the quantifiable variables should be included and in what form. In this study the research team decided that the variables selected for inclusion in the model should represent the best available estimates of legitimate determiners of faculty salaries. (For example, it would be possible to include in the data file the marital status of each faculty member on the assumption that this may be related to a person's salary. However, since marital status is not a legitimate determiner of an equitable salary policy by today's standards, it was not included even though it could be easily incorporated into the model.)

Legitimate Salary Determiners

The research team included the following variables as legitimate, possible determiners of faculty salaries: highest degree, prior experience, rank, academic discipline, and years at URI. (Other legitimate determiners might include quality of teaching, scholarship, and service, but these were not available in quantified form.) The assumption that salary should have some positive relationship to length of service is a common one. The basic rationale for the inclusion of each of the other variables is as follows:

Highest Degree. The possession of the appropriate terminal degree by a particular faculty member is an indication of the scholarly background the individual brings to the position. Legitimate expected duties of faculty members at a university include participation in scholarly activity designed to create additional knowledge in the professional field and to disseminate that knowledge to regional and national groups of professionals. Since acquisition of the knowledge and skills necessary to participate in such scholarly activity is typically an anticipated result of graduate and professional degrees, specifically the doctorate, the possession of such degrees is a likely indicator of knowledge and scholarly skills possessed by the faculty member and therefore a legitimate determiner of an equitable salary.

Prior Experience. Not all faculty members are hired immediately upon completion of their highest degree. Many come to the university with prior experience, for example, as a faculty member at another institution. We assumed that work experience after the receipt of the terminal degree was a legitimate determiner of an equitable salary. For example, we assumed that a department hiring an assistant professor with two years of prior experience at another university as an assistant professor might legitimately offer that person a higher starting salary than it would a beginning assistant professor who had just completed the doctorate.

We did not recognize or include experience prior to the completion of the terminal degree. (While such experience could have been estimated from the data file from which we were working, we did not include it because we did not consider it to be a good predictor of an individual's effectiveness as a faculty member.) In some disciplines a department may consider it necessary for potential faculty to have a certain amount of prior professional experience before applying for a faculty position. For example, a teacher education program typically requires faculty to have a minimum of three years of experience as an elementary or secondary school teacher. The rationale is that an individual closely involved with the training of teachers should have prior experience working as a teacher. This requirement is a minimum experience requirement that is attached to the position and is not necessarily reflected in higher salaries for the individuals involved. Thus the position requires two or three years prior experience as an elementary or secondary teacher (among other things) and pays a starting salary of, say, $13,000 per academic year. Under such a system an individual with fifteen years of classroom teaching experience would receive $13,000 for the same position since the additional years as a classroom teacher do not necessarily make a direct and important contribution to a person's performance as a faculty member. (This means, of course, that many individuals with a great deal of work experience prior to the receipt of the terminal degree may decide they cannot "afford" to apply for such a position. Others may decide that such a career shift offers enough rewards to compensate for the salary to make the change worthwhile to them.)

Rank. The inclusion of rank as a legitimate determiner of salary is seldom questioned in academic circles. (In order for salaries to be equitable between men and women, however, one must assure that promotions are awarded equitably among men and women. In our analyses we assumed that at URI men and women are promoted equitably. We did not test that assumption, although some descriptive data are included later.)

The ladder rank system of faculty promotions assumes that faculty of higher rank have more potential for and are performing at a higher level in the areas of teaching, research, and service. Including rank as a legitimate determiner of an equitable salary plan assumes that it is appropriate to reward this higher level of potential and performance with higher salaries.

Academic Discipline. It is generally recognized that faculty positions in some disciplines offer higher salaries than positions in other disciplines. We are assuming that, at least to some extent, this pattern is legitimate and may be part of an equitable salary plan. Starting salaries for URI faculty members (and for faculty at other universities) are established in part as a result of market factors. These market factors include the number of qualified people nationally available for the position and the salaries they could make in other academic and nonacademic positions. Market factors change over time; the post-Sputnik era was characterized by high salaries for well-trained physical scientists. The late 1960s saw a decreased emphasis on certain of the physical sciences, the increased availability of freshly trained scientists, and a depressed "market effect" in terms of what a university would have to pay a new Ph.D. faculty member in physical science.

Two departments in which "market effects" are now at least temporarily important are history and accounting. In certain areas of history important to the university, when a faculty position is advertised, the department can expect to hear from hundreds of qualified candidates with completed doctorates who are willing to start as assistant professors at approximately $13,000 per academic year. The accounting department, on the other hand, is presently in a state of continual search for qualified candidates. Because of the current demand, the department may find that it has to hire faculty members who have not yet completed the degree, and must pay them on the order of $18,000 per academic year as beginning assistant professors. This higher salary is necessary to attract good candidates with competing offers from other comparable universities or private enterprise.

If the university were not willing to accept the notion of legitimate difference in starting salaries between faculty from different disciplines, an appropriate starting salary would still have to be determined. To extend our example, one must ask whether beginning assistant professors with earned doctorates and no prior university experience should be paid starting salaries of $13,000 or $18,000. The former solution might well mean that the accounting department could find no good candidates for its vacancies, while the latter solution might lead to a situation in which the university had fewer faculty positions to fill in each department since most positions would cost more to fill.

We recognize that there are some dangers in the way we treated the assumption that discipline is a legitimate determiner of faculty salaries. For instance, if disciplines that are predominately male are paid more due to some prior discrimination while disciplines that are historically and predominantly female are paid less due to these same discriminatory practices, our analysis will mask that discrimination.

Again we recognize that whatever discriminatory market factors exist at URI may also exist at other universities. The effect of discipline shows up clearly in chapter 3. However, neither we nor the advocacy groups have gathered and presented data on the extent to which differential market factors are legitimate results of the economic system and the degree to which they reflect discriminatory practice.

Given these determiners, we will now proceed to the model development.

The Model

Within a particular rank an individual's present salary (SAL) is simply the sum of his or her starting salary (START) and all subsequent increments. The increments reflect experience (EXP). Therefore salary may be written

$$SAL = START + g(EXP) \qquad (9.1)$$

where g is a function.

Salaries in the United States have consistently increased since 1936 because of both productivity gains and inflationary pressures. For that reason a person's starting salary should be positively related to the year of initial appointment. This variable is entered into the analyses as

$$TIME = APPT - 1936 \qquad (9.2)$$

where APPT is the year of initial appointment. Thus TIME is interpreted as years since 1936.[1]

Experience (EXP) is defined as the number of years since the receipt of the final degree, unless the individual received his or her degree after being first appointed at URI. In this case EXP is simply the number of years at URI. Equation 9.2 therefore becomes

$$SAL = f(TIME) + g(EXP), \qquad (9.3)$$

where f is a function.

The functional form of equation 9.3 can be discussed in terms of its two additive components. The first term is a result of a growth economy and should appear as an exponential function; however, to preserve linearity in the coefficients a quadratic is chosen. Both linear and squared terms are expected to have positive coefficients (see figure 9-1). The second term is a result of the increasing value of an individual as experience is gained. However, it is generally

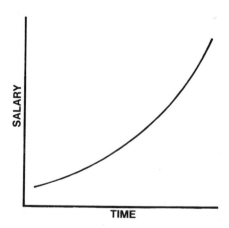

Figure 9-1. Quadratic Nature of the Relationship between Time and Salary.

believed (and the market reflects this) that the first five years of experience are more important than the next five. For this reason a quadratic functional form is chosen with the expectation that the squared term will enter the equation with a negative coefficient (see figure 9-2). Equation 9-3 then becomes

$$SAL = \gamma_0 + \gamma_1 \text{ TIME} + \gamma_2 \text{ (TIME)}^2 + \beta_1 \text{ EXP} + \beta_2 \text{ (EXP)}^2 \qquad (9.4)$$

where

$$\gamma_0, \gamma_2 > 0 \text{ and } \beta_1 > 0, \beta_2 < 0.$$

Starting salary also depends on market forces, that is, the opportunity cost of choosing an academic rather than an applied job. For example, one would expect universities to have to offer higher salaries to engineers than to English professors. Because this opportunity cost is difficult to quantify with the available set of data, the discipline (DISC) was entered as a series of dummy or shift variables.[2]

Finally dummy variables reflecting Ph.D. (PHD) and sex (SEX) are included. We expect the coefficient on the Ph.D. and rank variables to be positive but have no a priori expectations on the sex variable.

The resulting equation is

$$SAL = \beta_0 + \sum_{i=i}^{3} \delta_i RANK_i + \sum_{i=i}^{12} \alpha_i DISC_i + \gamma_1 \text{ TIME}$$

$$+ \gamma_2 \text{ TIME}^2 + \beta_1 \text{ EXP} + \beta_2 \text{ EXP}^2 + \lambda_1 \text{ PHD} + \lambda_2 \text{ SEX}$$

$$(9.5)$$

Estimation Results

Regression analyses included three definitions of salary as the independent variable. Salary refers to 1974-75 academic year salary for all 694 faculty members. Base salary is defined as 1974-75 salary minus any administrative supplements and merit, market, and inequity adjustments included as part of the 1974-75 contract settlement. Current salary is defined as 1974-75 academic year salary minus administrative supplement only.

Table 9-1, 9-2, and 9-3 contain the results of estimating equation 9.5 using ordinary least squares. All variables are of the expected sign and, with the exception of several disciplines and SEX, are significant at the 99 percent level. Although all three regression analyses indicate that women are *ceteris paribus* paid less than men, the difference is not statistically significant for any of the three definitions of salary.

Figure 9-2. Quadratic Nature of the Relationship between Experience and Salary.

Table 9-1
Ordinary Least-Squares Regression Analysis of Salary for All Faculty

Right-Hand Variable	Estimated Coefficient	t-Statistic
CONSTANT	7383.17	7.11
RESDEV	1227.34	2.33
LIBSCI	2239.00	2.55
ENGR	4081.70	7.59
HOMEC	1419.17	2.47
NURSE	2054.08	3.49
PHARM	1740.43	2.57
BUS	4017.68	7.12
OCEAN	1105.79	1.76
ARTSC1	1902.65	3.59
ARTSC2	1410.06	2.70
ARTSC3	1571.51	3.01
ARTSC4	877.37	1.79
ASSIST	1247.42	2.83
ASSOC	2951.59	6.03
FULL	7293.94	13.28
PHD	1579.41	6.75
TIME	−160.38	−2.45
TIME2	4.86	3.64
EXPER	408.20	8.54
EXP2	−6.24	−5.77
SEX	−353.66	−1.44

R-squared = 0.80.
Durbin-Watson statistic (adjusted for 0.0 gaps) = 1.97.
Standard error of the regression = 1987.76.
F-statistic $(21, 672)$ = 130.54.

Table 9-2
Ordinary Least-Squares Regression Analysis of Base Salary
for all Faculty

Right-Hand Variable	Estimated Coefficient	t-Statistic
CONSTANT	7061.46	6.59
RESDV	1386.28	2.55
LIBSCI	2520.30	2.79
ENGR	4337.20	7.80
HOMEC	1689.74	2.85
NURSE	2072.51	3.41
PHARM	1913.47	2.74
BUS	4208.72	7.23
OCEAN	1366.17	2.10
ARTSC1	2150.04	3.93
ARTSC2	1626.98	3.02
ARTSC3	1787.83	3.32
ARTSC4	1040.10	2.06
ASSIST	1068.49	2.35
ASSOC	2667.36	5.28
FULL	7043.88	12.43
PHD	1579.99	6.55
TIME	−158.01	−2.34
TIME2	4.93	3.57
EXPER	401.89	8.15
EXP2	−5.99	−5.37
SEX	−480.30	−1.90

R-squared = 0.79.
Durbin-Watson statistic (adjusted for 0.0 gaps) = 1.95.
Standard error of the regression = 2050.69.
F-statistic $(21, 672)$ = 122.41.

The equations were then reestimated within each rank (the rank shift variables were, of course, omitted). Table 9-4 presents the results of the sex variable only. These differences should be interpreted as average differences rather than figures that are true in each case. These analyses indicate that although women are paid less than men at the assistant, associate, and full professor ranks, when all factors included in the data file are taken into consideration, the difference is significant only at the assistant professor rank. The largest SEX coefficient is at the full professor rank (consistent with other studies). However, there is so much variation around the average that the difference is not significant at that rank. The average underpayment at the rank of assistant professor is smaller but quite significant, indicating a clear general tendency within the rank.

Residuals

The model-building/regression analysis approach can also be used to define underpayment. If one accepts inequalities produced by the capitalist system as

Table 9-3
Ordinary Least-Squares Regression Analysis of Current Salary for All Faculty

Right-Hand Variable	Estimated Coefficient	t-Statistic
CONSTANT	7365.93	7.19
RESDEV	1239.47	2.39
LIBSCI	2254.14	2.61
ENGR	4054.47	7.63
HOMEC	1402.60	2.48
NURSE	2076.77	3.58
PHARM	1690.24	2.53
BUS	3964.24	7.13
OCEAN	1111.70	1.79
ARTSC1	1841.09	3.52
ARTSC2	1421.36	2.76
ARTSC3	1543.73	3.00
ARTSC4	889.40	1.84
ASSIST	1249.10	2.87
ASSOC	2911.28	6.03
FULL	7237.16	13.36
PHD	1570.09	6.81
TIME	−136.93	−2.12
TIME2	4.24	3.22
EXPER	397.15	8.43
EXP2	−6.01	−5.64
SEX	−331.94	−1.37

R-squared = 0.80.
Durbin-Watson statistic (adjusted for 0.0 gaps) = 1.96.
Standard error of the regression = 1960.27.
F-statistic $(21, 672)$ = 133.19.

normal and justified, then all the variables included in equation 9.5, with the exception of SEX, measure inequality rather than inequity. For example, the fact that a member of the English department is paid less than an equivalent member of the business college does not necessarily mean that the former is underpaid.

Equation 9.5 was reestimated omitting SEX. The resulting equation furnishes a formula or rule for calculating an individual's *proper* salary in which discipline, rank, experience, time, and terminal degree are all included. The difference between the actual salary and the proper (or fitted salary then becomes a measure of underpayment. Note that this residual reflects everything that is not included in the regression. Some of these missing variables (such as research output) may be legitimate determiners of equitable salaries; others may not. These residuals are graphed for men and for women in figure 9-3. As the data in figure 9-3 indicate, the range of residuals is rather large among both men and women faculty.

Table 9-4
SEX Coefficients, Standard Errors, and *t*-Ratios for Regression Analyses within Rank Using Three Definitions of Salary

		SEX Coefficient			Standard Error			*t*-Ratio		
		Base	Current	Salary	Base	Current	Salary	Base	Current	Salary
Instructor	(*n* = 27)	940	917	917	859	836	849	1.09	1.10	1.08
Assistant	(*n* = 223)	−569	−463	−484	211	197	203	−2.69	−2.35	−2.39
Associate	(*n* = 234)	−434	−326	−351	378	359	366	−1.15	−0.91	−0.96
Full	(*n* = 210)	−1399	−1092	−1112	1038	997	1003	−1.35	−1.09	−1.11
All faculty	(*n* = 694)	−480	−332	−354	252	241	244	−1.91	−1.38	−1.45

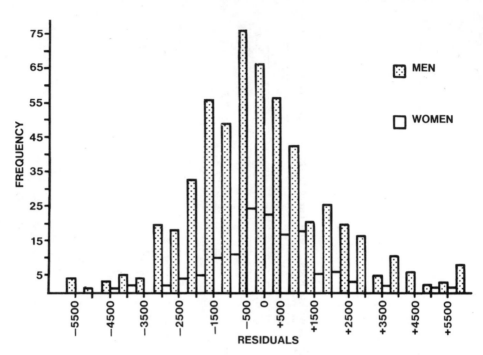

Figure 9-3. Histogram of Men's and Women's Salary Residuals

Whether the inclusion of omitted variables (assuming they could be adequately quantified) would alter the conclusions depends on the distribution of these variables across sex. For example, if males do more research than females, the underpayment of women is greatly exaggerated in the analysis. However, if the converse is true, the analysis is understating the degree of sex discrimination. Finally, if there is no tendency for either sex to engage in more or less research than the other, the results would not be altered by the inclusion of the missing variable. Technically the coefficients and their standard errors would remain unbiased. It is because of the possible consequences of missing variables that the statistical analysis was supplemented with a case-study approach.

Some Indications of the Future

Within rank the only statistically significant differences among men's and women's salary when degree, discipline, and experience since the terminal degree are taken into account are among assistant professors. Our attempts to explain this difference were unsuccessful.

The typical pattern in academe is for the differences among men's and women's salaries to increase with rank and experience. Therefore it is surprising to discover that significant differences exist among men and women at the assistant professor rank even when degree, experience, and discipline are taken into account. To determine whether this pattern was continuing among newly hired faculty a cursory study of the new hires at the university for the 1976-77 year was undertaken. Using the regression equation, we predicted a salary for each newly hired continuing appointee. Note that the predicted salary for the new hires is of theoretical interest only, since their actual salaries are two years in advance of the actual salaries in the population. Thus because of inflation we would expect, on the average, that using the equation would yield positive residuals for the new hires. Table 9-5 summarizes our findings for the new hires compared with the rest of the university.

The data in table 9-5 indicate that the hiring pattern for 1976-77 was consistent with previous years in terms of the proportion of men and women hired and in terms of the proportion of men and women hired with the doctorate in hand. Among the twenty-nine men and eight women hired in tenure-track positions for 1976-77, men are paid an average of $458 more, after rank, terminal degree, prior experience, and discipline are taken into account. Thus even among the newest hires there are unexplained differences in salaries using our equation. Whether these differences are due to legitimate factors not included in our equation (such as past record or promise of scholarly productivity) or whether they are discriminatory in nature is not fully explained by the data at hand.

To learn more about the relative contributions of variables about which little is known in a quantified sense, the research team decided to gather data on scholarly productivity from a random stratified sample of faculty members. The sample was the same as that employed in chapter 11 by John Long and, as he explains, was chosen to represent the broad range of salary residual categories.

Table 9-5
Comparison of 1974-75 Faculty Characteristics with 1976-77 New Hires

| | *1974-75 Faculty Population* | | *1976-77 New Hires* | |
	Men	*Women*	*Men*	*Women*
Number	555	139	29	8
Percentage	75	25	78	22
Percentage with Ph.D.	80	40	83	38
Average rank[a]	2.05	1.32	1.45	0.50
Salary				
Average academic	$18,250	$14,531	$17,238	$12,131
	(1974-75)	(1974-75)	(1976-77)	(1976-77)
Average residual	00.00	$332	$636	$178

[a]0 = instructor, 1 = assistant professor, 2 = associate professor, 3 = full professor.

Sampling Scholarly Production

Equitable salaries for faculty may be determined by a number of characteristics. Since our population data set did not contain information about qualitative variables, we were interested in gathering at least a sample of such data through the interview process.

Qualitative information that would be considered valid determiners of equitable faculty salaries would be essentially the same information used to make qualitative decisions about faculty with regard to promotion and tenure. That is, we assume that the quality of a person's teaching, research, and service are legitimate determiners of an individual faculty member's salary, that a faculty member who is outstanding at teaching, research, and service should legitimately be paid more than one who is poor in these areas, all other things being equal.

Within our resource limitation for conducting the study, we decided to limit the gathering of qualitative information to the area of scholarly productivity. We defined scholarly productivity as the number of outcomes: articles, books, poems, paper presentations, and so forth. There were several reasons for this decision: First, we had a limited amount of time to do the study. Second, we had to rely on self-report data. Third, the number of scholarly productions is easily reported and counted on a uniform basis and easily translated into an index about which one can make qualitative judgments. This would not be true for any similar self-report indices for teaching or service. Finally, other studies in which researchers wished to gather information about faculty productivity have used similar methods. Most of these count the number of books and articles. We feel that our index is better than a mere counting of books and articles since it allows more discipline-appropriate distinctions (that is, faculty in an art department may list one-person shows; faculty in English may list the publication of poems and short stories).

The use of our scholarship index to measure productivity should not be interpreted to mean that quality of scholarly output is unimportant. On the contrary, when decisions are made about individual faculty, quality in all areas of achievement is an important variable.

The stratified sample of forty faculty whom we interviewed completed self-reports of their scholarly activities that were based on categories widely accepted as the material outcomes of scholarly activities. The categories ranged across all types of scholarship activity and were not limited to those that result in a printed product. The interviewee was also free to supply additional items that did not fit the categories supplied.

To reduce the scholarship data into a single index, we chose weights for each category after several slightly overlapping categories were collapsed. The weights employed are listed in table 9-6. These weights were arrived at after the research team discussed the effort and evaluative prestige of each contribution to

Table 9-6
Weights Employed in Generating the Scholarship Index

Variable Category	Weight
Books, both sole- and team-authored	8
Monographs and chapters in books	3
Refereed journal articles	5
Nonrefereed journal articles	2
Newsletter articles	1
Edited readings or collected works	4
Grant application authorship	1
Grant application funded	2
Regional and national paper presentations	2
Short stories or poems published	4
One-person shows	4
Reviews and miscellaneous equivalents	1

scholarship. Differences in weights proposed were resolved by using the median value proposed. The resulting compound was calculated for all forty of the interviewees' scholarship record sheets. The range was from a low of zero to a high of 369. For simplicity the index was divided into five ranges in order to smooth a rather uneven distribution. The ranges and the approximate percentages of the sample in each are displayed in table 9-7.

To determine the extent of relationship of the scholarship index with salary, rank, residual, and other variables presumed or suspected to be related to scholarly production, several cross tabulations and correlations were calculated. The first of these is presented in table 9-8.

It is clear from the table 9-8 that scholarship is positively associated with rank which, of course, has been shown to be a strong determiner of salary. Virtually all the assistant professors were in the two lowest categories of scholarship; most of the full professors were in the two highest categories; the associates were spread across the distribution but had more in the lower categories than did the full professors and more in the upper categories than did the assistant professors. While it is reassuring to find the more productive

Table 9-7
Scholarship Ranges and Percentage Distribution of Interviewees in Each Range

Scholarship Index Range	Percentage of Sample
I: 0-12	32.5
II: 13-35	17.5
III: 36-100	22.5
IV: 101-150	12.5
V: 151-369	15.0

Table 9-8
Cross Tabulations of Scholarship Index with Rank of Interviewee:
Frequency and Percentages

Scholarship Index Range	Rank			
	Inst.	Asst.	Assoc.	Full
I	0	9 (69.2)	3 (30.0)	1 (5.9)
II	0	3 (23.1)	4 (40.0)	0
III	0	1 (7.7)	0	8 (47.1)
IV	0	0	2 (20.0)	3 (17.6)
V	0	0	1 (10.0)	5 (29.4)

scholars in the upper ranks, confirming the widely held assumption that scholarship is associated with advancement in rank, it is not very instructive to limit our inspection to this relationship. A fuller understanding of the impact of scholarship is assisted by inspecting the correlations between scholarship and residual and both actual and predicted salary. The correlation between scholarship and residual is more important because it will help explain the remaining differences in salary after rank, degree, years at the university, and so forth, have been taken into account. These correlations appear in table 9-9.

The correlation between scholarship and salary, both actual and predicted, is reassuringly high. Correlation with residual, however, is low, suggesting that the relationship is confounded with rank, degree, and the other variables entered into the prediction model.

Because of our interest in the various relationships among the interview variables, and particularly the relationships between the scholarship variables and the other variables of this study, a table of correlations, table 9-10, was generated.

While the correlations between the scholarship index (V21) and all the remaining scholarship variables, except newsletter articles, are understandably high and positive, the correlation between that index and number of years at the university is not. This lack of correlation suggests that the length of time a

Table 9-9
Correlations between Scholarship Index and Salary, Predicted Salary,
and Residual for the Interview Sample

Variable	Correlation with Scholarship Index
Actual salary	0.65[a]
Predicted salary	0.57[a]
Residual	0.19

[a]$p < 0.001$.

Table 9-10
Selected Zero Order Correlations among Interview and Scholarship Variables

	V3 Sex	V4 Residual	V6 Years at URI	V9 Books published	V10 Monographs/chapters	V11 Refereed articles	V12 Nonrefereed articles	V13 Newsletter articles	V14 Edited readings	V15 Grant applications	V16 Grant funded	V17 Paper presentations	V18 Short stories/poems	V20 Reviews/misc.
V4	0.09													
V6	-0.02	-0.06												
V9	-0.18	0.23	0.06											
V10	-0.32[a]	0.29[a]	0.15	0.74[b]										
V11	-0.39[a]	0.08	0.09	0.36[b]	0.44[b]									
V12	-0.31[a]	0.04	0.15	0.32[a]	0.40[b]	0.25								
V13	-0.04	-0.07	0.09	0.00	-0.02	-0.02	0.23							
V14	-0.13	0.22	0.11	0.91[b]	0.75[b]	0.38[b]	0.35[a]	0.06						
V15	-0.47[a]	0.00	0.05	0.05	0.26	0.59[b]	0.32[a]	-0.09	0.08					
V16	-0.42[a]	0.03	-0.03	0.14	0.32[a]	0.47[b]	0.43[b]	-0.13	0.10	0.79[b]				
V17	-0.27[a]	0.24	-0.01	0.42[b]	0.46[b]	0.64[b]	0.42[b]	0.12	0.38[b]	0.34[a]	0.35[a]			
V18	0.10	0.19	0.25	0.02	-0.02	-0.02	-0.11	0.13	-0.04	-0.09	-0.13	0.25		
V20	0.14	0.15	0.09	0.18	0.06	0.03	-0.06	-0.03	-0.06	-0.02	0.10	0.32[a]	0.50[b]	
Scholarship index V21	-0.41[b]	0.19	0.14	0.61[b]	0.66[b]	0.88[b]	0.48[b]	0.07	0.59[b]	0.58[b]	0.56[b]	0.81[b]	0.18	0.23

[a] $p < 0.05$.
[b] $p < 0.01$.

person spends at the university is not directly related to scholarly production. While scholarship has been shown to be positively and strongly related to rank (r = 0.58), this relationship suggests that scholarship is recognized in initial rank and subsequent promotions and is relatively independent of length of service. It further suggests that persons are either scholars or nonscholars and that time does not seem to mediate differences. Both conclusions are speculations from partial data, but they demonstrate interesting, albeit incidental, implications of the data.

The correlations of the sex variable (V3) with all the remaining variables have to be viewed with some qualifications. First, the sex variable is a twofold categorization and second, the remaining variables are largely continuous ones. Therefore these correlations should be seen only as indicative, and the reader should look to cross tabulations and arithmetic means for indications of sex differences in scholarship. A negative correlation with any of the other variables nonetheless indicates that the males possessed more of the trait underlying the variable. For most of the scholarship variables and the scholarship index, the correlation with sex was negative and in most cases significant. A way to confirm this is by inspection of the means for each of these variables for both men and women. Table 9-11 displays most of the same variables with means for men, women, and the entire sample.

It seems clear from table 9-11 that the men in the interview sample were far

Table 9-11
Descriptive Statistics for Interview and Scholarship Variables for Men and Women

	Means		
Variable	Men	Women	Total
Actual salary	$18,888	$15,941	$17,654
Predicted salary	18,993	16,149	17,803
Residual	−105	−208	−149
Books published	0.67	0.19	0.48
Chapters and monographs published	2.00	0.25	1.30
Refereed articles published	8.37	1.63	5.70
Nonrefereed articles published	3.04	0.44	2.00
Newsletter articles published	1.71	1.44	1.60
Edited/collected readings published	0.42	0.00	0.25
Grant applications authored	6.46	0.56	4.10
Grant applications funded	3.88	0.38	2.48
Regional/national papers presented	7.50	3.50	5.90
Short stories/poems published	0.42	1.00	0.65
One-person shows	0.00	0.00	0.00
Reviews/miscellaneous	1.50	3.00	2.10
Scholarship index	95.00	28.00	68.20

more productive in scholarship than were the women in the sample. While the relationship of scholarship with residual may appear weak (table 9-9, $r = 0.19$), the differences between men and women in scholarship may explain much of the remaining differences after factors in rank, age, degree, discipline, and other variables have been taken into account.

If a scholarship index had been calculated for all the faculty, the regression might have produced an even smaller residual difference between men and women or even reduced that difference to zero. Teaching performance can be considered an equal, if not stronger, determiner of salary and promotion; and if it is, one can reasonably assume that it would have a similar relationship to the residual and might help further explain differences. It is unlikely that qualitative information on teaching is used in setting initial salaries. Consequently it probably has far less effect than scholarship on overall salaries.

The baseline of all scholarship is the education credential itself. Possession of the doctorate weighs heavily in the setting of initial salary and is claimed to be indicative of the potential to engage in significant original scholarship. In gross figures, men at the University of Rhode Island are twice as likely to possess the doctorate as are women. A more careful analysis of the proportion of men and women with and without the doctorate is given in table 9-12.

Inspection of table 9-12 suggests that not having a doctorate slows the advancement of both men and women. It seems, in fact, to affect men more adversely than women, although this difference may be mostly disciplinary; that is, it is more likely that a woman may advance without the doctorate because she is more likely to be in a discipline (at least at the University of Rhode Island) in which the doctorate is not necessary to advancement. Overall, however, the table must be interpreted with care. Longer time in rank at the assistant professor level can be interpreted as a negative judgment; but longer time in rank at the full professor level may not be so interpreted because there is no higher rank to be promoted to. Inspection of the two intermediate ranks, however, suggests that not possessing the doctorate results in a longer stay at that rank. However, women do not seem to be as significantly affected at these ranks.

Table 9-13 shows the relationship between holding the doctorate and the arithmetic mean of the scholarship index for each group.

Table 9-13 seems to suggest that while males are more active in scholarship than females with comparable levels of education, both groups are considerably less active than their colleagues when the doctorate is not part of their professional dossiers. A serious qualification to interpretation of these data is that, since women tend to be in disciplines that do not require the doctorate as the minimal qualification for membership, there may be a lesser expectation for performance in scholarly activities. Females in the sample with doctorates tended to outperform both males and females without doctorates, but they did not do as well as males with doctorates.

Table 9-12
Average Years in Rank for Men and Women

	Current Rank							
	Instructor		Assistant Professor		Associate Professor		Full Professor	
	Ph.D.	*No Ph.D.*	*Ph.D.*	*No Ph.D.*	*Ph.D.*	*No Ph.D.*	*Ph.D.*	*No Ph.D.*
Men								
Number	2	7	112	38	153	47	180	16
Average number of years	1	3.6	4.2	5.2	4.1	9.1	7.6	5.3
Women								
Number	0	18	24	49	19	15	12	12
Average number of years	—	3.06	4.3	4.2	4.1	5.3	6.5	2

Table 9-13
**Mean Scholarship Index for Men and Women, with and without
the Doctorate**

Group	Mean Scholarship	n
Total interview sample	68.2	40
Males with doctorate	122.7	17
Females with doctorate	46.3	9
Males without doctorate	27.9	7
Females without doctorate	4.4	7

Summary of Findings

The major findings of the study are summarized:

1. The average male faculty member is paid $18,250 ($N$ = 555) for an academic year, while the average female faculty member (N = 139) is paid $14,532.
2. Women faculty are older than men faculty at each rank; overall the averages are nearly the same (men = 44.8 years; women = 44.1 years).
3. The average length of service for women faculty was 8.8 years; for men the average was 11.1 years.
4. At each rank men are more likely than women to possess the doctorate. Among the total faculty, 80 percent of the men and 40 percent of the women have doctorates.
5. The median rank for male faculty is associate professor; the typical female faculty member is approximately one-third of the way between assistant and associate professor.
6. The average male professor is paid $332 more than the average female professor when rank, discipline, and experience since the final degree are held constant. That difference is not statistically significant.
7. The merit, market, and inequity adjustments that were part of the 1974-75 contract reduced the average difference between men's and women's faculty salaries by $148 when rank, discipline, experience, and final degree were held constant.
8. Comparisons of salaries within academic rank when final degree, experience, and discipline are held constant indicate that only at the assistant professor rank is there a statistically significant difference between the average male faculty member and the average female faculty member. That average difference was $463.
9. The newest hires at the university are much like previously hired faculty. Men outnumber women by about three to one and are twice as likely to

have the doctorate. Men in 1976 were hired at an average salary that was $458 higher than women when rank, discipline, experience, and final degree were held constant. Men were hired at a median rank between assistant professor and associate professor; women's median rank at time of hiring was halfway between instructor and assistant professor.

10. According to data supplied by an interview sample, the typical male faculty member was three times as likely as the typical female faculty member to have published a journal article and twice as likely to have presented a paper at a regional or national conference.

11. Data on a sample of faculty indicate that scholarly productivity is strongly related to rank and to salary.

12. Men and women spend about the same amount of time in rank before promotion to assistant professor. However, for the period between 1970 and 1976, women spent about a year longer in rank before being promoted to associate professor and almost four years longer in rank before being promoted to full professor. The extent to which these differences are directly related to differences in scholarly productivity cannot be determined from the data available for this study.

Policy and Procedural Recommendations

Because of the wide distribution of residuals (unexplained differences between actual salary and salary predicted on the basis of rank, discipline, experience, and highest degree) and because both men and women appeared at almost every interval of the distribution of residuals, the recommendation of a simple formula adjustment to any group to eliminate salary inequities does not seem to be the fairest solution. Instead the research team reported a series of policy recommendations designed to eliminate inequities in individual salaries among both men and women and to establish procedures that would decrease the likelihood of future inequities. Any institution contemplating procedures for ameliorating inequities should consider the following recommended procedures based both on our analyses and interviews at the University of Rhode Island and our knowledge of the literature and the machinations of higher education.

1. *A permanent salary review panel or board should be established to study each alleged case of inequity and to make recommendations about appropriate adjustments.* The panel should be composed of representatives from academic affairs, personnel, the faculty, and affirmative action. The group should review in-depth studies of individual cases of alleged inequity by conducting interviews with the individual involved as well as his or her department chairman and by inspecting appropriate data contained in a salary equity analysis report (this should be the panel's first order of business) and should make recommendations about the resolution of each case. The panel should also propose policies that go

beyond the scope of these recommendations to the continued development and implementation of equitable salary policies. The panel should spend at least a semester developing procedures for inequity adjustments. The establishment of these procedures is particularly important, for the resolution of individual cases may not change differences between particular groups; in fact, group averages may appear even further apart when individual adjustments have been made. Procedures must be established a priori because the community must be willing to accept certain tolerable inequalities as just and defensible after the existing inequities are adjusted and new operating policies are put into effect to prevent new inequities. The panel should assume responsibility for or have access to periodic updates of the types of analyses described in this chapter. These updates should occur at least every three years to insure reasonably current comparative information.

2. *The review panel should consider cases of inequity among both men and women and cases involving alleged inequities for a variety of possible reasons, including discriminatory hiring practices, changing market conditions, and long-standing promises that have never been fulfilled.* This recommendation is based on our collective belief that unexplained variance in individual salaries for both men and women is due to a number of factors. Only after a careful review of a particular case, taking into consideration the salary and professional history of the individual, qualitative performance factors, and legitimate market factors within disciplines, can an equitable recommendation be made in an individual situation. The consequences of each adjustment should be reviewed so that solving one inequity does not unwittingly create several more.

3. *The salary equity analysis report should be widely distributed to the campus community, including special interest groups, for their use in making specific recommendations about individual salaries. Recommendations should not be accepted for classes of individual faculty members nor without the express consent of faculty members recommended for salary review.* The resolution of individual cases of inequity should be based on careful review of specific situations with input from the individual requesting an adjustment and the recommendations of the department chairman and the dean concerning the appropriate resolution of the request. The review should include the following information:

Professional and salary history of the individual.

A salary "residual" (the unexplained part of the individual's salary not necessarily resulting from inequitable treatment). While this is an important piece of information, in no case should the residual alone be the basis for a salary adjustment.

The rationale for the requested adjustment.

The recommendation of the department chairman and the dean, which should include a qualitative assessment of the individual's performance as a faculty member.

4. *Each faculty member should receive a letter informing him or her of the salary equity analysis report and of the opportunity for a salary review and the rationale by which the panel will conduct reviews.*

5. *More control should be used in the establishment of beginning salaries.* An acceptable range of starting salaries for each position should be set in a careful and systematic way that involves making the decision before the job is advertised. Specifically we recommend that a beginning salary (or alternate beginning salaries depending on possession of the appropriate qualifying degree, rank, and so forth) be established by the department and approved by the dean (and the academic affairs office in a multicollege structure) before the position is posted. Permission to make offers for starting salaries outside the agreed-upon range should be obtained in advance and only for the most exceptional circumstances.

6. *Administrative or special responsibility supplements should be used as term-of-office stipends for extra responsibilities.* Often a faculty member is hired at a higher-than-normal salary because the position includes responsibilities such as being the department chairman or starting a new academic or research program, and when the individual relinquishes those extra duties, there is no appropriate reduction in salary. Many salary equity analyses show that past administrative experience is a significant contributor to higher salaries.

Positions with responsibilities clearly other than those of a regular faculty member should be carefully reviewed before it is advertised to establish a salary structure that describes what the position would pay without those extra duties and the extra payment for assuming the additional duties. If the person, for whatever reason, continues in a faculty position without assuming those additional responsibilities, the supplement would be relinquished. This last feature should be specified in the letter of initial appointment.

7. *Each faculty member, upon initial appointment, should receive official notification of (a) initial salary conditions including any special supplements due to extra responsibilities; (b) rank or salary contingencies and how those contingencies will be executed (for example, "promotion to assistant professor, at no increase in salary, upon receipt of doctoral degree"); and (c) expectations of the position in terms of teaching, research, and service.* Such a letter would be useful in protecting the individual from unkept promises that may result from a change in administration, evaluating faculty claims that certain duties (such as conducting research or participating in institutional governance) were not specified when the individual was hired, and providing a useful solution when an individual's appointment includes extra duties for which a term-of-office administrative supplement is given.

8. *Initial salaries should take market conditions among disciplines into account by having initial salary requests by department include normative data on the profession involved (starting salaries from other comparable institutions hiring faculty at the same rank and degree requirements).* Full justification should be given for any first appointment above the average for that rank. A vote by department faculty to help set starting salary, prior to posting, may be useful to assure faculty awareness of new faculty salaries.

9. *Every possible effort should be made to hire new faculty at salaries comparable to recent hires in the same department with the same experience, rank, degree, and responsibilities.* Our interviews revealed several cases of faculty who believed that those hired after them in comparable circumstances were hired at higher salaries; our population data support this impression. This situation leads to poor morale among those hired previously. Among the steps that might be taken to avoid such a situation are the following.

When the coming year's salary is unknown at the time new faculty are being hired, new faculty should be hired at a temporarily lower salary that would be subject to some further increase when the final salaries have been negotiated for all other faculty.

For cases in which market conditions shift rapidly, the salary review panel should hear "class-action" requests that might, in extreme cases, recommend salary increases for several current faculty whose salaries have become inequitable.

10. *The institution should review the faculty status of the individuals assigned to the library and other special-function faculty "equivalents."* Some quasi faculty are granted faculty titles at salaries below regular faculty of comparable age and experience. When little is done to establish the institution's expectations of them as faculty members, teachers, and researchers, an apparent inequity is created.

Both the institution and the individuals involved might be better served by including them in another, more appropriate employee group without faculty titles or faculty expectations, avoiding what may appear to be a salary inequity.

Following these steps can yield major reductions in perceived inequities.

Notes

1. Many studies use age rather than time. In a cross-sectional study, it is impossible to determine ex post facto which specification is correct. We felt that time rather than age was the logically correct specification.

2. Disciplinary codes are as follows: RESDEV resource development (agriculture); LIBSCI library science; ENGR engineering; HOMEC home economics;

NURSE nursing; PHARM pharmacy; BUS business; OCEAN oceanography; ARTSCI1 humanities; ARTSCI2 social sciences; ARTSCI3 natural sciences; ARTSCI4 applied and professional studies, including education, physical education, and dental hygiene. The dummy code is library faculty membership. Other variable codes are ASSOC associate professor rank; ASSIST assistant professor rank; FULL full professor rank. The dummy code in rank is instructor. PHD holds the doctorate or equivalent; TIME year of appointment minus 1936; TIME2 the quadratic term for time; EXPER number of years since the award of the doctorate or the number of years since initial appointment, whichever is greater; EXP2 the quadratic term for EXP; SEX sex.

References

Abramson, Joan. *The Invisible Woman.* Washington, D.C.: Jossey-Bass, 1975.

Bayer, Alan E., and Astin, Helen S., "Sex Differentials in the Academic Reward System." *Science* 188 (May 23, 1975):796-802.

Carnegie Commission on Higher Education, *Opportunities for Women in Higher Education: Their Current Participation, Prospects for the Future, and Recommendations for Action.* New York: McGraw-Hill, 1973.

Centra, John A. *Women, Men, and the Doctorate.* Princeton, N.J.: Educational Testing Service, 1974.

Darland, M.G., Dawkins, S.M., Lavasich, J.L., Scott, E.L., Sherman, M.E., and Whipple, J.L., "Application of Multivariate Regression to Studies of Salary Differences between Men and Women Faculty." in *Proceedings of the Social Statistics Section,* Washington, D.C., American Statistical Association, 1973, pp. 120-132.

Dorfman, Robert, "Two Steps Backward: Report on the Economic Status of the Profession, 1974-75," *AAUP Bulletin* 6 no. 2 (August 1975):118-124.

Kieft, Raymond N., "Are Your Salaries Equal?" *College Management* 9, no. 23 (April 1974):23.

Lester, Richard A., "The Equal Pay Boondoggle," *Change* no. 7 (September 1975):38-43.

National Center for Education Statistics, "Salaries, Tenure, and Fringe Benefits of Full-Time Instructional Faculty, 1975-76," preliminary report, 1976.

**Part III
Some Dissenting Views
on Multiple Regression
and Statistical
Analysis**

10 Procedures for the Detection and Correction of Salary Inequities

Michael H. Birnbaum

This chapter presents criticisms of the usual regression analysis, as exemplified in the other chapters. A statistical paradox implies that in the absence of discrimination, women are expected to earn less than men with the same qualifications (years of experience, scholarly record, teaching performance) and simultaneously to be underqualified relative to men of the same salary. Therefore, before one can charge systematic discrimination, women must be shown not only to be underpaid relative to men of the same qualifications but also to have higher qualifications than men of the same salary. Hypothetical data, constructed without assuming any discrimination, were analyzed to show how the standard multiple regression analysis could yield the inappropriate conclusion of systematic sex bias. Two studies that had found sex bias on the basis of multiple regression were reanalyzed to show that there was no evidence of discrimination in one case and evidence of discrimination in the other.

In the second part of the chapter Birnbaum argues that an equation predicting existing salaries as a function of criteria such as years, rank, and publications may yield an unfair measure of merit by perpetuating past inequities. As a solution, he suggests that the merit equation should predict salaries that are judged equitable. In the third part of the chapter Birnbaum discusses methods for distributing raises and shows that three common methods increase or leave unchanged group and individual salary inequities. He proposes a new method which can eliminate both group and individual inequities in a few years. The proposed method eliminates group differences in salary (for the same merit) and merit (for the same salary) without requiring that individuals be identified by group.

In recent years scholars have shown increased interest in how the meager funds appropriated for higher education are distributed. This chapter discusses problems with methods recently advocated for detecting and correcting salary inequities. I will show that the only way to satisfy the Equal Pay Act of 1963 is to pay everyone according to merit. It follows that merit must be measured with great precision; accordingly methods for improving this measurement are

Thanks are due Lloyd Humphreys, Lawrence Jones, Michael Levine, Barbara Mellers, and Ledyard Tucker for suggestions.

suggested. I demonstrate that raises computed as percentage increases based on merit actually increase group differences and individual inequities and present a superior algorithm for assigning salary increases according to merit. This method eliminates sex differentials and individual inequities without violating the Equal Pay Act or psychological considerations of equity.

Analysis of Group-Related Inequities

Most investigators agree that it would be inappropriate to argue for the existence of sex discrimination in university salaries if men make more money on the average than women, since men tend to have published more, have greater seniority and experience, and score higher on other objective merit criteria. Multiple regression promises to allow comparisons between groups that statistically hold constant the differences on measurable merit variables.

Typical Regression Analysis

Current uses of multiple regression for investigating salaries may be misleading, and actions based on the results of such analyses may be misguided or even illegal. A typical application is as follows. First, a regression equation is developed to predict the salaries of white males from a linear composite of measurable merit indices such as number of journal articles published, number of books, ratings of teaching, and years of experience. Then the salaries of females (or other groups) are computed from the equation and compared with their actual salaries. Some have suggested that if the actual salary of a female is far below its predicted value, the salary should be increased (Nevill, 1975; Scott, 1977; Braskamp, Muffo, and Langston, 1978).

The typical finding is that women are lower in both salary and indices of merit than men. Even after regression analyses are performed, the average salary of women is found to be lower than that of comparable men. In other words, sex is still a predictor of salary after multiple merit variables have been used (Bayer and Astin, 1975; Bergman and Maxfield, 1975; Braskamp, Muffo, and Langston, 1976; Ferber and Loeb, 1977; Gordon, Morton, and Braden, 1974; Johnson and Stafford, 1974; Katz, 1973; Koch and Chizmar, 1976; Malkiel and Malkiel, 1973; Reagan and Maynard, 1974; Scott, 1977; Tuckman and Tuckman, 1976).

The regression coefficient for group membership, the average difference in salary between groups holding merit constant, is generally interpreted to represent inequity. Various substantive interpretations have been given, including sex discrimination, differential mobility (hence differential use of counteroffers to raise salary), market factors, differential criteria of evaluation for different groups, and so forth.

Another Type of Analysis

Another analysis studies people of the same salary and compares their indices of merit. People of the same salary should be of equal merit, according to this paradigm. Suppose that with salary held constant, women were lower in merit than men? This might generally be believed to indicate reverse discrimination, possibly arising from affirmative action. Neither of these analyses can be interpreted so simply. It may be possible that with merit held constant, women earn less; yet for the same data women may have fewer publications and less experience than men of the same salary.

Galton's Paradox

The reader who is puzzled by this possibility is in good company. Legend has it that no less a genius than Francis Galton was puzzled by a similar problem when he compared the heights of children and their parents (Miller, 1962). Galton found that the sons of tall fathers were taller than average but shorter than their fathers; he first thought perhaps people were getting smaller. Then he found that the sons of short fathers were shorter than average but taller than their fathers and thought that perhaps everyone was approaching the same height, regressing to the mean. Then he found that the fathers of short sons were taller than the sons and that the fathers of tall sons were shorter than their sons. How can it be that fathers of tall sons are shorter than their sons and, simultaneously, that sons of tall fathers are shorter than their fathers? Galton was as puzzled about this seeming contradiction as people are today when they study salary inequities. How can it be that with qualifications held constant women receive less salary than men and that with salary held constant women are less qualified?

The answer to both questions lies in part in understanding that when correlations between variables are less than perfect, the least-squares prediction of one variable based on another is always close to the mean of the predicted variable. One cannot simply invert the regression equation for predicting fathers from sons to obtain the equation for predicting sons from fathers. The relevance of these arguments to the study of salaries can be made explicit by considering the implications of a one-factor theory of salary and merit that assumes no sex discrimination.

A Null Hypothesis for Equity Research

An individual's salary is said to be equitable if it has the same standing in the distribution of salaries as the individual's quality relative to the distribution of quality. If two people have the same quality they should have the same pay; if two people differ in quality, the person with the greater quality should receive greater pay.

Before one charges group-related inequity, one should show that the data permit rejection of the null hypothesis that groups are treated equivalently. I will show that multiple regression outcomes taken as evidence of inequity are predicted by the theory that salaries depend only on quality.

Suppose that there are three variables, sex (X), salary ($\$$), and a weighted composite of measured merit indices, called merit (M) for short. (The nature of the merit variable is not crucial to this argument. It may be defined by armchair considerations, derived from multiple regression analysis of the majority group, or bootstrapped from judgments of hypothetical faculty.) Suppose that one factor, quality (Q), underlies all the intercorrelations among these three variables. In other words, the same equations predict salary and merit from quality, $\hat{\$} = f(Q)$, $\hat{M} = g(Q)$, independent of sex. Suppose for simplicity, that the equations are linear.

$$z(\$_i) = q_\$ z(Q_i) + s_i$$
$$z(M_i) = q_m z(Q_i) + m_i \qquad (10.1)$$

where $z(\$_i)$ and $z(M_i)$ are standard scores of salary and merit for case i; that is,

$$z(\$_i) = (\$_i - \mu_\$)/\sigma_\$$$
$$z(M_i) = (M_i - \mu_M)/\sigma_M$$

μ and σ represent mean and standard deviation; $z(Q_i)$ is the standard score of quality for case i; $q_\$$ is the correlation between merit and quality. The residuals s_i and m_i are uncorrelated with quality.

If the residuals s and m are uncorrelated with each other and are uncorrelated with sex, a theory of discrimination would not be required in order to reproduce the correlations among the observed variables. It follows that the intercorrelation between each pair of variables can be expressed as the product of the correlations between the variables and quality. That is, for $k \neq j$ the correlation, ρ_{kj}, is given by the product

$$\rho_{kj} = q_k q_j \qquad (10.2)$$

We can represent the three variables in the following arrangement.

$$
\begin{bmatrix} q_\$ \\ q_M \\ q_X \end{bmatrix}
\begin{bmatrix} q_\$ & q_M & q_X \end{bmatrix} =
\begin{array}{ccc}
\$ & M & X
\end{array}
\begin{bmatrix} - & q_\$ q_M & q_\$ q_X \\ - & - & q_X q_M \\ - & - & - \end{bmatrix}
\begin{array}{c} \$ \\ M \\ X \end{array}
$$

where the diagonal and the lower triangular portion of the matrix have been left blank for clarity.

If the correlations among the variables can be accounted for by the extent to which the variables correlate with quality, one would not need to postulate a discrimination or inequity factor to account for the correlation between salary and sex. The model does not require the assumption or denial of any causal relationships among the variables. Sex differences in quality may be due to social or biological causes or may represent chance differences not worthy of causal interpretation; the statistical analysis requires no causal assumptions, nor does it test them. Unless the variables have been experimentally manipulated, it is premature to make causal interpretations of regression equations.

Implications. The null hypothesis of equity makes specific predictions for multiple regression analyses. The least-squares regression coefficient for sex in predicting salary (in standardized scores) is given by the equation

$$\beta_{\$X \cdot M} = \frac{\rho_{\$X} - \rho_{XM}\, \rho_{M\$}}{1 - \rho_{XM}^2} \tag{10.3}$$

where $\beta_{\$X \cdot M}$ denotes the beta weight for sex (X) in a standardized multiple equation predicting salary $(\$)$, where merit (M) is included in the prediction equation. This coefficient, $\beta_{\$X \cdot M}$, is directly proportional to the difference in salary between males and females, with merit held constant. Using substitutions from equation 10.2, which assumes that quality is the only factor, we have

$$\beta_{\$X \cdot M} = \frac{q_\$ q_X - q_X q_M q_M q_\$}{1 - (q_X q_M)^2} = \frac{q_\$ q_X (1 - q_M^2)}{1 - (q_X q_M)^2} = \frac{\rho_{\$X}(1 - q_M^2)}{1 - q_X^2 q_M^2} \tag{10.4}$$

Equation 10.4, which assumes no discrimination, implies the following conclusions.

1. If there is no correlation between sex and quality, then the coefficient for sex will be zero; that is, if $q_X = 0$, then $\beta_{\$X \cdot M} = 0$. Under this model, ρ_{XM} would also be zero, as would $\rho_{X\$}$.
2. If the relationship between measured merit and quality is perfect, then the regression coefficient for sex would be zero; that is, if $q_M = 1$ then $\beta_{\$X \cdot M} = 0$). (The distinction between measured merit M and quality is an important one. Number of publications, for example, would only be moderately correlated with a person's scholarly contribution. Most persons would agree that the number and quality of publications are imperfectly correlated.)
3. The regression coefficient, $\beta_{\$X \cdot M}$, will have the same sign as the correlation between sex and salary. It will be smaller in absolute value if the correlation between measured merit and quality is improved.

Thus *without postulating any sex-related inequity, this simple model predicts that under realistic conditions* (sex differences in merit and imperfect predictions of salary from merit), *the regression coefficient for sex is predicted to be nonzero and of the same sign as the correlation between sex and salary.*[1] Therefore the finding of past researchers that women are paid less than men of equal merit is *not* conclusive evidence against the equity null hypothesis.

The equity null hypothesis has other testable implications that permit a more appropriate analysis in the search for evidence of discrimination. Suppose we look at merit, holding salary constant. The coefficient for sex in this equation, $\beta_{MX \cdot \$}$, can have stronger interpretations when related to $\beta_{\$X \cdot M}$. The equation for this coefficient is as follows.

$$\beta_{MX \cdot \$} = \frac{\rho_{MX} - \rho_{\$M}\rho_{\$X}}{1 - \rho_{\$X}^2} \tag{10.5}$$

According to the equity null hypothesis (equation 10.1),

$$\beta_{MX \cdot \$} = \frac{q_M q_X - q_\$ q_M q_\$ q_X}{1 - (q_\$ q_X)^2} = \frac{q_M q_X (1 - q_\$^2)}{1 - (q_\$ q_X)^2} = \frac{\rho_{MX} (1 - q_\$^2)}{1 - q_\$^2 q_X^2} \tag{10.6}$$

Equation 10.6 implies that if quality explains the intercorrelations among the variables, then the regression coefficient for sex in predicting merit with salary in the equation should have the same sign as the correlation between measured merit and sex. Thus, if men have higher merit than women of the same salary, it might appear to constitute evidence of discrimination in favor of females, but it is not necessarily, no more than a positive $\beta_{\$X \cdot M}$ implies discrimination in favor of males.

Equations 10.4 and 10.6 show that the sex differences in regression intercepts depend on the loadings of the predictor variables. The salary differences with merit held constant can be zero only if measured merit correlates perfectly with quality; otherwise it varies inversely with q_M. Ironically *the worse the measurement of merit in a study, if one assumes no discrimination, the greater the apparent discrimination when measured by multiple regression.* The merit difference with salary held constant can be zero only if salary correlates perfectly with quality (if $q_\$ = 1$).

Diagnostic Test for Inequity. Here then is a proper method for establishing the presence of sex-based inequity. If one group is simultaneously paid less than members of the other group with the same merit *and* has greater merit than persons of the other group with the same salary, one can reject the equity model. The equity model implies that the effect of sex in both regressions should have the same sign as the simple correlations with sex. If the signs of these constants reverse, then another factor (such as discrimination) will be needed to account for the correlations.

Numerical Examples

Table 10-1 shows hypothetical values of quality, salary, and merit for males and females generated without assuming any sex-related inequity. Sex is a binary-valued variable (0 = female, 1 = male). The mean value of quality is greater for males than females, but there is considerable overlap in the distributions. The residual scores for salary and merit, E_1 (0 or 1) and E_2 (0, 1, or 2), are factorially combined with each other and with each value of quality. Thus E_1 and E_2 are uncorrelated with each other, with quality, and with sex. These error scores are analogous to m and s in equation 10.1, except they are not in a standard score equation. The values of salary ($) and merit ($M$) are generated by raw-score forms of equation 10.1.

$$\$_i = 13 + 2(Q_i + E_{1i})$$

$$M_i = 10 + 10(Q_i + E_{2i})$$

(10.7)

where salary is in thousands of dollars and merit is a composite [such as 2 × (years of experience) + (publications in excellent journals), for example].

The correlation between sex and salary is 0.46, between sex and merit 0.40, and between salary and merit 0.67. These correlations can be reproduced by the products of the correlations of the variables with quality: 0.52, 0.88, and 0.76 for sex, salary, and merit, respectively.

Since there is no discrimination, one might have supposed that with merit held constant there would be no difference in salary. Instead, the difference is as expected on the basis of regression. For example, consider the salaries of persons of merit equal to 30. For females, these would include case numbers 3, 6, 8, 11, 13, 16, with salaries of $13,000, $15,000, $15,000, $17,000, $17,000, and $19,000. The average salary for these females is $16,000. Males with merit equal to 30 include cases numbered 20, 23, 25, and 28, with salaries of $15,000, $17,000, $17,000, and $19,000, respectively, with a mean of $17,000. Thus with merit held constant at 30, males are paid $1,000 more than females on the average.

Paradoxically, a similar analysis of merit yields the seemingly contradictory conclusion that females have less merit than males of the same salary. For example, the mean merit of females earning $15,000 is only 25, compared with 30 for the males. The mean merit of women earning $19,000 is only 40, compared with 45 for the men.

Figure 10-1 plots the hypothetical data of table 10-1. Salaries are plotted

Table 10-1
Hypothetical Values of Quality, Salary, and Merit for Females and Males

			Females								Males				
Case	Sex	Quality	Errors		Salary	Merit	Case	Sex	Quality	Errors		Salary	Merit
i	X	Q	E_1	E_2	$a	M^b	i	X	Q	E_1	E_2	$a	M^b
1	0	0	0	0	13	10	19	1	1	0	0	15	20
2	0	0	0	1	13	20	20	1	1	0	1	15	30
3	0	0	0	2	13	30	21	1	1	0	2	15	40
4	0	0	1	0	15	10	22	1	1	1	0	17	20
5	0	0	1	1	15	20	23	1	1	1	1	17	30
6	0	0	1	2	15	30	24	1	1	1	2	17	40
7	0	1	0	0	15	20	25	1	2	0	0	17	30
8	0	1	0	1	15	30	26	1	2	0	1	17	40
9	0	1	0	2	15	40	27	1	2	0	2	17	50
10	0	1	1	0	17	20	28	1	2	1	0	19	30
11	0	1	1	1	17	30	29	1	2	1	1	19	40
12	0	1	1	2	17	40	30	1	2	1	2	19	50
13	0	2	0	0	17	30	31	1	3	0	0	19	40
14	0	2	0	1	17	40	32	1	3	0	1	19	50
15	0	2	0	2	17	50	33	1	3	0	2	19	60
16	0	2	1	0	19	30	34	1	3	1	0	21	40
17	0	2	1	1	19	40	35	1	3	1	1	21	50
18	0	2	1	2	19	50	36	1	3	1	2	21	60
Mean		1	0.5	1	16	30			2	0.5	1	18	40

$a = 13 + 2 \times$ (quality $+ E_1$).
$^bM = 10 + 10 \times$ (quality $+ E_2$).

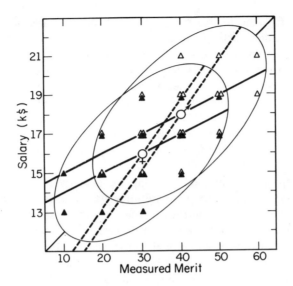

Note: Solid triangles represent females; open triangles represent males. Points that would have coincided have been shifted slightly. Centroids for the two groups are represented by the sex symbols. Solid lines represent the least-squares regression equation predicting salary from sex and merit. Dashed lines show least-squares regression lines predicting merit from salary and sex. The ellipses are drawn for artistic purposes, to help distinguish the scatter of points for the two groups.

Figure 10-1. Salary Plotted against Merit for Hypothetical Data of Table 10-1.

against merit, with solid triangles for females and open triangles for males. The sex symbols represent the centroids for the two groups. Ellipses have been drawn to help identify the two groups. Note that the male scatter plot can be produced by shifting the female scatter plot up along the 45° diagonal axis in figure 10-1. The solid regression lines represent the least-squares equation for predicting salary from merit and sex. In raw-score form the equation is

$$\hat{\$}_i = 13 + 1X_i + 0.1M_i \tag{10.8}$$

where $\hat{\$}_i$, X_i, and M_i are raw scores for case i, with predicted salary $\hat{\$}_i$ measured in thousands of dollars. Note that females ($X = 0$) are paid $1,000 less on the average than males ($X = 1$).

The dashed lines in figure 10-1 show the least-squares predictions of merit from sex and salary. The equation is as follows.

$$\hat{M}_i = -28.18 + 2.73X_i + 3.64\$_i \tag{10.9}$$

where $\hat{M}_i$ is predicted merit. Note that women ($X = 0$) have less merit (2.73 less) than men of the same salary. This example shows that it would have been inappropriate to argue for sex-related inequity on the basis of a difference in salary between women and men of the same merit.

Figure 10-1, representing a situation without a sex-related inequity, shows what can happen when salaries are adjusted on the assumption that females should be paid the same as the average male of the same merit. Eleven females fall below the males' regression line for salary (upper solid line). Presumably these eleven could have their salaries adjusted upward. However, note that four of these eleven cases have less merit than the average male of the same salary. To adjust their salaries and not those of the corresponding males would not be fair or legal.

A more appropriate method for adjusting inequitable salaries would be to identify persons of both sexes who are underpaid relative to colleagues of the same merit *and* have greater merit than colleagues of the same salary. Cases 3, 9, 15, 21, 27, and 33 satisfy these criteria (lowest and rightmost points in figure 10-1). Note that in this example, which assumed no discrimination, an equal proportion of males and females are identified as deserving salary adjustments.

To understand how a sex inequity would be detected, add $1,000 to all the men's salaries in table 10-1 and figure 10-1. The males' centroid in figure 10-1 would move above the dashed line representing the females' merit line. Thus males would now have less merit than females of the same salary—clear evidence against the equity null hypothesis. Indeed the least-squares regression equation for merit becomes

$$\hat{M}_i = -28.18 - 0.91X_i + 3.64\$_i \qquad (10.10)$$

The coefficient for sex is now negative, showing that women have greater merit than men of the same salary. Therefore equation 10.1 could be rejected. Under these conditions nine females would be identified as both high in merit and underpaid, cases 2, 3, 6, 8, 9, 12, 14, 15, and 18. The same three males as before (21, 27, and 33) would be underpaid by the same standard.

As a final point, consider the effects of adding $1,000 to the salaries of all the women in table 10-1 and figure 10-1. Multiple regression would detect no difference in intercepts between males and females, predicting salary from merit. However, examination of figure 10-1 shows that the difference in merit for persons of the same salary would approximately double! Of persons who have the same salary, the average male will have 3.18 additional years of experience (or 6.36 additional publications) than the average female of the same salary. The elimination of a sex differential in salary in this way has the unfortunate effect of increasing the sex differential in merit for persons of the same salary.

Table 10-2 shows a hypothetical correlation matrix consistent with the absence of sex-based inequality. Notice that each off-diagonal intercorrelation can be expressed as a product of loadings of the variables on quality (sex (X) is defined so that males have a higher score). Note that the two regression analyses

Table 10-2
Hypothetical Intercorrelations and Quality Loadings for
Equitable Example

	Quality Model				Off-Diagonal Correlation Matrix		
	$	M	X		$	M	X
$	[0.8	[0.8	0.9	0.3]	=	0.72	0.24	$
M	0.9						0.27	M
X	0.3]							X

would lead to the seemingly paradoxical conclusions that women are paid less than equally qualified males ($\beta_{\$X \cdot M} = 0.05$) but are less qualified than equally paid males ($\beta_{MX \cdot \$} = 0.05$).

Table 10-3 shows a hypothetical correlation matrix in which two of the three entries are the same as in table 10-2, yet discrimination exists. The second factor represents discrimination. Note that the 0.24 correlation between sex and salary cannot be explained in terms of quality but depends on discrimination as well. In this case women are paid less than men of the same merit ($\beta_{\$X \cdot M} = 0.18$), but women have greater merit than men of the same salary ($\beta_{MX \cdot \$} = 0.10$).

The one-factor model implies that the ratio of the correlation between sex and salary to the correlation between sex and merit is bounded by the correlation between salary and merit and its reciprocal. The relationship is as follows.

$$\rho_{M\$} \leqslant \frac{\rho_{X\$}}{\rho_{XM}} \leqslant \frac{1}{\rho_{M\$}} \tag{10.11}$$

since

$$q_M q_\$ \leqslant \frac{q_\$}{q_M} \leqslant \frac{1}{q_M q_\$}$$

Table 10-3
Example of Evidence for Inequity

	Two-Factor Model						Off-Diagonal Correlation Matrix		
						$	M	X	
$	[0.8	0.4]	[0.8	0.9	0.1]	=	0.72	0.24	$
M	0.9	0	0.4	0	0.4]			0.09	M
X	0.1	0.4]							X

When the ratio equals $\rho_{M\$}$, then $q_M = 1$; when it equals $1/\rho_{M\$}$, then $q_\$ = 1$. The greater the correlation between merit and salary, the smaller the region in which the one-factor model would be acceptable. In table 10-3, $\rho_{\$X}/\rho_{MX} = 2.67$, which is outside the region from 0.72 to 1.39; therefore the one-factor model cannot describe the data of table 10-3.

Illustrative Empirical Examples

Figure 10-2 shows reanalyses of two studies conducted seven years apart at the University of Illinois. The raw data for these studies are not available, and some ingenuity was required to recover the information in figure 10-2 from the limited statistics presented in the original reports. Figure 10-2A shows 1976 salaries for 153 females and 119 males "matched" by department (Braskamp, Muffo, and Langston, 1976). The solid lines are the regression lines predicting

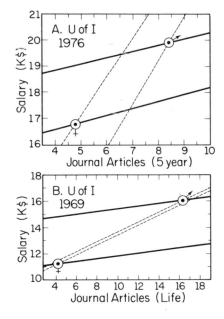

Note: (A) Solid lines for 1976 salaries show that males are paid more than females with equal number of publications in five years. Dashed lines show that males have published more articles per five years than females of equal pay. Based on statistics reported by Braskamp, Muffo, and Langston (1976). There is no evidence in panel A to reject the equity null hypothesis. (B) 1969 salaries are inconsistent with the one-factor hypothesis. Based on statistics reported by Katz (1971).

Figure 10-2. Reanalyses of Two Salary Studies at the University of Illinois, 1976 and 1969.

salary from number of publications with a separate line for each sex. The vertical spread between the curves shows that on the average males are paid about $2,000 more than females with the same number of publications. The dashed lines predict number of publications (per five years) from salary—the horizontal spread between the curves shows that females publish about two fewer articles per five years than males who receive the same salary. One would expect women in a discriminatory situation to have published more than men with the same salaries. Figure 10-2A thus shows no evidence to reject the one-factor null hypothesis; there is no evidence for group-related inequity. Similar conclusions were reached using a composite index that included linear and nonlinear functions of eleven indices of merit, including years of professional experience and grant dollars.

Ironically the University of Illinois decided on the basis of the typical but incomplete analysis to provide special funds as equity adjustments for females only. This action, even had the data shown evidence of discrimination, would apparently violate the Equal Pay Act of 1963, since underpaid males were not eligible for the equity review.

Figure 10-2B plots a reanalysis of data presented by Katz (1971), a portion of which were published later (Katz, 1973). If the regression lines for males and females are assumed to be linear and parallel, these 1969 salaries are inconsistent with the equity null hypothesis. Extrapolation of the dashed curves shows that the merit line for females lies to the right of that for males. Thus females published half an article more than males of comparable salary in 1969. Analyses of composites including other merit variables yielded similar conclusions.

In sum, when data of two studies were reanalyzed using the diagnostic test, the conclusions changed in one case and not in the other. Thus there is a real danger that studies claiming to have demonstrated systematic sex bias could have their conclusions altered by the appropriate reanalysis.

Group versus Individual Inequity

The preceding arguments show that in the absence of sex discrimination, one should expect men to receive higher average salaries than women of the same merit. Similarly one should expect men to have greater merit than women of the same salary. Most persons feel that such results (as in figure 10-2A) are evidence of inequity—and they are right. Individual inequities, produced by a lack of perfect correlation between salary and merit, produce these paradoxical group differences. There is no way to eliminate these paradoxical group differentials in merit and salary without either eliminating group differences in both merit and salary (fire women of low merit or men of high merit until there is no sex difference in merit?) or produce a perfect correlation between measured merit and salary.

If the Equal Pay Act of 1963 requires that men and women of identical merit receive equal pay and also that men and women of equal pay have equal merit, then the law requires a perfect monotonic relationship between salary and merit. Otherwise individual inequities within sex will result in apparent evidence of sex discrimination. Administrators must face the challenge of measuring merit in a precise way and of paying everyone, regardless of group membership, according to the same standards. If the universities do not establish academically sound definitions of merit, the government may force its own definitions on the universities.

If salaries and measured merit are to be perfectly correlated, then the measurement of merit will have to be improved. The next section describes how merit can be measured, and the third section shows how to raise salaries to eliminate both group and individual inequities.

Improving Measures of Merit

Modeling Existing Salaries

Multiple regression of existing salaries may be used to identify persons of both sexes who fall short of the regression equation, for possible correction. This proposal asks that everyone be paid according to whatever equation best predicts existing salaries. It is reasonable to suspect that a multiple linear combination of merit indices has a higher correlation with quality than does salary, so this proposal has some appeal.

By deriving the definition of merit from existing salaries, however, multiple regression may perpetuate past inequities. For example, if "good old boys" earn more and publish less, publications may turn out to have a negative weight in predicting salaries if scholars and good old boys are mixed together in the analysis.[2] Yet most people feel that it would not be equitable to define merit with a negative weight for publications, so that a person receives less for publishing more.

Katz (1971) found that psychologists at the University of Illinois received $209 per year more for each article published in an excellent journal and $33 less per year for each article in a less-than-excellent journal, although both types of publications were positively correlated with salary. Such an effect may represent a "correction" for quality of publications: faculty who have a low threshold for submitting papers for publication may have large numbers of both types of articles, and the quality of their excellent journal publications may be uneven. It may also represent one of the mysterious ways that multiple regression can select weights when variables are highly correlated.

It does not seem appropriate to allow the multiple regression equation to select optimal weights for predicting current salaries if the weights cannot be defended as leading to psychologically "just" measures of merit for all cases.[3]

Clinically Judged versus Statistically Computed Merit

It could be argued that intuitive ratings of quality made by a committee or by a department chairman should be used instead of computations based on measured merit. One may think that a person could take into account quality differences that are difficult to measure. However, when clinical judgments and objective calculations are compared, objective calculations have been found to be superior in reliability and validity (Sawyer, 1966; Dawes, 1976).

What makes a department head think that he or she can arrive at a better assessment of someone's scholarly contribution by reading a vita and letters of evaluation than by counting the number of publications in refereed journals? Editors and reviewers spend many hours studying each paper before accepting it. By taking a journal's reputation into account, as Katz did (1973), the objective formula can process the previous judgments of others who are usually more suited to make the evaluation in a reliable fashion. Dawes (1976) has called the judge's (in this case, the head's) confidence in his or her own information-processing capacities a "cognitive conceit." As bad as objective indices of merit are for measuring quality, more than sixty studies suggest that clinical judgments would be worse (Dawes, 1976; Sawyer, 1966).

Assessments of merit based on functions of objective criteria have, in addition to their greater reliability and validity, four other advantages over clinical evaluations. First, the employee will not feel that the assessments are affected by the personal biases of his colleagues. Second, the employee will not be surprised by the assessment. Third, the employee will understand how to raise the assessment. Fourth, objective measures are easier to document in lawsuits or government actions in connection with the Equal Pay Act.

Bootstrapping Subjective Judgments of
Equitable Salaries

A system that uses judges to derive merit measures that are fair and uses an objective formula to measure merit for individuals seems to combine the best of both worlds. Such a system can be achieved by means of a variation of what has been termed bootstrapping in the judgment literature.

The procedure would be as follows. First a committee would meet to discuss merit and decide which variables should contribute to the definition of merit. Then a number of hypothetical faculty profiles would be constructed from a factorial design of merit values, and faculty judges would propose fair salaries for these hypothetical faculty. These judges would have to ask themselves questions such as, Should a person with one year of experience and five excellent publications earn more than a person with five years of experience and one excellent publication? Of course, different judges would be expected to have different opinions. For each hypothetical faculty member, the median salary judgment should be calculated. (Galton pointed out that the median is a good number to use for such purposes, since half the judges advocate paying the person more and half say less.)

Then procedures for model diagnosis can be used to define a function F to best predict the median judgments,

$$\hat{M} = F(X_1, X_2, X_3, \ldots, X_p) \tag{10.12}$$

where $\hat{M}$ is the calculated merit from merit variables X_1, X_2, X_3, $\ldots$, X_p that best predicts the median "fair salary" judgments; F is the function that transforms, weights, and combines the merit variables.

Three Faces of Equity

The function F relating median judged salary to components of merit can be profitably decomposed into three psychological processes (see, for example, Birnbaum, 1974a, 1974b), as follows.

$$M = J[I(H_1(X_1), H_2(X_2), \ldots)] \tag{10.13}$$

where $\hat{M}$ is the predicted judged value, J is an equity judgment function that matches salary to merit, I is an integration function that combines measures of merit to form an overall assessment of merit, and the H_i functions are transformations relating subjective merit to each of the objective measures of merit.

Each of these processes can be illustrated by the following examples:

1. The question of the linearity of H for publications is illustrated by the question, Should the effect of the difference between five publications and ten be equivalent to the difference between ten and fifteen?
2. The I function, which combines the (transformed) measures of merit can be illustrated by questions involving trade-offs of values among sets of variables, for example, Should the difference in merit between five and ten publications be the same for all levels of experience? Should a person with one year of experience and five publications be paid more than a person with five years of experience and one publication?
3. Once merit is defined, there remains the problem of establishing an equitable distribution of salaries. The assignment of salaries to merit is accomplished by means of J. Most persons would agree that J should be a monotonic increasing function, and many would also argue that differences in salary should be proportional to differences in merit. But many J

functions are compatible with these ideas, even subject to the constraints that J be linear and that the total of salaries is fixed by the budget. For example, everyone could be paid the mean salary plus αZ_M where α is any constant and Z_M is the Z-score for merit. With α close to zero, however, it would seem unfair that large changes in merit would not be rewarded by large changes in salary. The cross-modality matching of salary to merit is a complicated process worthy of empirical investigation. For example, should a person with ten publications and two years of experience be paid twice as much as someone with five publications and one year of experience?

Example

Table 10-4 shows a simple example of the type of analysis that can be performed in order to measure merit. Entries in table 10-4 represent judgments of a single faculty member who named a fair salary for each of twenty-five hypothetical new faculty members described by years of experience and publication rate. It was then discovered that the equation

$$\text{Merit} = 14 + 0.25 \text{ years} \times (1 + \text{publication rate}) \qquad (10.14)$$

described the judgments well, except for the person with twenty years of experience and 3.0 publications per year, where a "mistake" of $10,000 was made. For this case the equation seems better than the judge.

According to this judge, it is better to have published forty articles with ten years of experience than to have published fifteen articles in thirty years. A person with ninety publications and thirty years of experience "deserves" to earn about twice as much as a person with twenty publications and ten years of experience, even though the objective indices are more than three times as great.

This approach could be extended to include all the relevant variables such as service and teaching. This problem will not be an easy one to solve, but its

Table 10-4
Judged Salaries "Deserved"

Average Publications per Year	Years of Experience				
	1	5	10	20	30
0.5	14	15	17	21	25
1.0	14.5	16	19	24	29
2.0	14.8	18	22	29	36
3.0	15.0	19	24	24	44
4.0	15.2	20	27	39	51
5.0	15.5	22	29	44	60

solution is long overdue, on the basis of both equity considerations and legal requirements.

Once the equation for merit has been developed, it is possible to calculate the salary deserved for each individual. The problem then is how to distribute salary increases according to merit to achieve equity.

Methods for Salary Increment to Achieve Equity

This section describes three general models for distributing salary according to merit. The three models have different implications for the growth of salary as a function of time, for considerations of equity, and for the Equal Pay Act.

Salary equity is defined as follows. Equity exists in a community if for all members of the community, salary is a perfect monotone function of merit. The present definition is a more general and weaker statement than previous definitions considered by psychologists (Adams, 1965; Anderson, 1976; Harris, 1976; Walster, Bersheid, and Walster, 1973), which assert that salary should be proportional to merit.

Merit is an inclusive term that is presumed to depend on a variety of factors including years of professional experience, quality of scholarly contribution, service, impact, and recognition.

Inequity is said to exist if two individuals of identical merit receive different salaries, if two individuals of different merit receive the same salary, or if a person with lower merit receives a higher salary than a person of higher merit. Inequities are produced not only when an individual's salary jumps because an offer from an outside institution is matched but also when someone increases in merit. The person who started with higher merit and stopped working will tend to have a higher salary under most systems than a person of equal merit who increased his merit slowly. Inequities are also produced by hiring persons of lower merit at higher salaries.

In all the following models let M_i = merit for individual i, $\$_i$ = salary for individual i for the present year, and Δ_i = the salary increment to be given this year (next year's salary = $\$_i + \Delta_i$).

Absolute Increment System

The absolute increment is a monotone function g of merit.

$$\Delta_i = g(M_i) \tag{10.15}$$

Present salary has no effect on the raise, except inasmuch as merit and salary are correlated. Two people with the same merit (even with different salaries) receive the same raises. This system neither removes nor inflates differences in salary between two persons of the same merit.

Relative Merit System

In the widely used relative merit system the percentage increase depends on merit, where $p(M_i)$ is the percentage raise.

$$\Delta_i = p(M_i)\$_i \tag{10.16}$$

Note that the increase is the product of merit and salary. If two people have the same merit but different salaries, the relative system gives a larger raise to the person with the higher salary. This system tends to inflate inequitable differences in salary between persons of equal merit.

An Equitable System

The following system can reduce and eventually eliminate inequities. The equation is as follows.

$$\Delta_i = a\left[f(M_i) - \$_i\right] + g(M_i) \tag{10.17}$$

where f and g are monotonic functions; a is a constant (the ratio of new budget money divided by total inequities). The expression $a[f(M_i) - \$_i]$ has the effect of reducing inequities in salary. If two people have equal merit but different salaries, the person with the lower salary receives the greater raise in this system. If two people have equal salaries and different merits, the person with the greater merit receives the greater raise. The expression $g(M_i)$ gives an additional increment due to merit only. When $f(M_i) = \$_i$ for all individuals, the system becomes formally equivalent to both absolute and relative merit systems, and equity is achieved. The advantage of equation 10.17 is that it can reduce inequities over time and can eventually eliminate inequities.

A simple version of equation 10.17 would let g be a linear function, that is, $g(M_i) = bM_i$. The values of a and b can then be specified as follows.

$$a = A/\Sigma\left[f(M_i) - \$_i\right] \tag{10.18}$$

$$b = B/\Sigma M_i \tag{10.19}$$

where A = total new budget money available for equity reduction, B is the total to be used for purely merit raises, and $\Sigma[f(M_i) - \$_i]$ is the total amount of money required to give each person a salary equal to $f(M_i)$.

Comparison of the Systems

Table 10-5 shows a comparison of the three systems for the hypothetical employees of table 10-1. For this example assume that merit has been measured precisely and is very close to the concept of quality discussed in the first two parts of this chapter. The present salaries and merits are from table 10-1, with $g(M_i) = M_i/35$. The future salaries represent salaries three years later with budget increases of 8 percent per year. For the equity method the initial equity line was defined as follows : $f(M_i) = 13,500 + 205M_i$. The original salaries showed considerable evidence of individual inequities, since persons of equal merit receive different salaries (cases 9 and 34) and persons of lower merit (case 34) receive higher salaries than persons of greater merit (case 15). The initial correlation between salary and merit is only 0.67.

The relative system increases inequities. In three years the difference in salary between cases 34 and 9, who are equal in merit, has grown from $6,000 to $7,700. Since case 9 is female, she could contend that discrimination caused the salary difference to increase. Indeed the relative system increased the average sex difference in salary, holding merit constant at 1.14, from $1,000 to $1,300. Procedures such as those described by Braskamp, Muffo, and Langston (1976) would perhaps raise her salary by means of a special equity payment. Unfortunately case 21, who is equal in merit to cases 9 and 34 but who is male, would not be considered for an equity increase under a system like that at Illinois. Of course case 21 could sue the university for raising the salaries for females only, in violation of the Equal Pay Act, and he would probably win (see the case of *Regents* v. *Dawes*, 1975).

The absolute system is preferable to the relative system, since differences in salary between persons of equal merit are not increased. Absolute raises do not reduce inequities, however. The $6,000 difference between cases 34 and 9 (not to mention case 21) would remain constant under the absolute system.

The equity system eliminates all inequities in three years without lowering anyone's salary. Note that persons of the same merit have identical salaries at the end of three years. For example, cases 9, 12, 14, 17, 21, 24, 26, 29, 31, and 34, who are equal in merit, now receive $22,400 per year, irrespective of their starting salaries. Were new faculty of lower merit hired at high salaries, were outside offers to be matched, or were some faculty to raise their merit, it would take longer than three years to achieve equity.

To study the power of the equity system, a very inequitable hypothetical department was used. In this department salaries for persons of the lowest merit ranged from $14,000 to $26,000; for persons of the highest merit, they ranged from $17,000 to $47,000. Using 60 percent of the new budget for A in equation 10.18, 40 percent for pure merit (B in equation 10.18), and assuming 8 percent budget increases per year eliminated all inequities in six years. Thus the equity method is a procedure that can realistically correct an unfair salary distribution.

Table 10-5
Comparison of Methods for Adjusting Salaries

			Females							Males		
				Future Salary[a]							Future Salary[a]	
Case	Merit g(M)	Present Salary	Relative	Absolute	Equity[b]	Case	Merit g(M)	Present Salary	Relative	Absolute	Equity[b]
1	0.28	13	13.9	14.2	16.1	19	0.57	15	17.1	17.5	18.3
2	0.57	13	14.8	15.5	18.3	20	0.86	15	18.2	18.8	20.4
3	0.86	13	15.8	16.8	20.4	21	1.14	15	19.3	20.0	22.4
4	0.28	15	16.0	16.2	16.1	22	0.57	17	19.3	19.5	18.3
5	0.57	15	17.1	17.5	18.3	23	0.86	17	20.6	20.8	20.4
6	0.86	15	18.2	18.8	20.4	24	1.14	17	21.9	22.0	22.4
7	0.57	15	17.1	17.5	18.3	25	0.86	17	20.6	20.8	20.4
8	0.86	15	18.2	18.8	20.4	26	1.14	17	21.9	22.0	22.4
9	1.14	15	19.3	20.0	22.4	27	1.43	17	23.2	23.3	24.6
10	0.57	17	19.3	19.5	18.3	28	0.86	19	23.0	22.8	20.4
11	0.86	17	20.6	20.8	20.4	29	1.14	19	24.4	24.0	22.4
12	1.14	17	21.9	22.0	22.4	30	1.43	19	26.0	25.3	24.6
13	0.86	17	20.6	20.8	20.4	31	1.14	19	24.4	24.0	22.4
14	1.14	17	21.9	22.0	22.4	32	1.43	19	26.0	25.3	24.6
15	1.43	17	23.2	23.3	24.6	33	1.72	19	27.6	26.6	26.7
16	0.86	19	23.0	22.8	20.4	34	1.14	21	27.0	26.0	22.4
17	1.14	19	24.4	24.0	22.4	35	1.43	21	28.7	27.3	24.6
18	1.43	19	26.0	25.3	24.6	36	1.72	21	30.5	28.6	26.7
Mean		16	19.5	19.8	20.4			18.0	23.3	23.0	22.4

[a]Future salaries assume 8 percent budget increases for three years.

[b]Equity values computed using 60 percent of budget for equity and assuming initial equity line: $f(M) = 13500 + 7143g(M)$.

Affirmative Action or Reverse Discrimination?

Recent papers have advocated procedures to be applied only to certain members of specified groups. Such procedures violate both the commonsense concept of justice and the Equal Pay Act. Such procedures are doomed to failure in any case. The procedures advocated elsewhere cannot adjust salaries in table 10-1 so that males and females of the same merit have the same mean salary *and* persons of the same salary have the same mean merit unless all individual inequities are eliminated.

The equity method described here seems vastly preferable to such discriminatory affirmative action techniques, because it treats members of all groups equally yet eliminates group differences in salary (for fixed merit) and merit (for fixed salary). Table 10-5 shows that one can eliminate group differences without discriminating. This method may prove extremely useful for calculating timetables for affirmative action goals that can be realized without injustice. Unless salaries are raised on the basis of equity considerations for all individuals, however, nondiscriminatory mechanisms such as percentage merit increases will inflate individual inequities and paradoxical group differences.

Summary

If one group scores lower on both salary and measurable merit and if regression analysis indicates that members of this group have lower salaries than predicted from measured merit variables, one should not automatically infer group-related inequity. Any individual whose salary falls short of that of colleagues with equal merit *and* whose merit exceeds that of colleagues with equal salary seems most deserving of an equity adjustment. It is not possible to eliminate paradoxical group differences in salary (holding merit constant) and merit (holding salary constant) without eliminating all individual inequities, that is, without producing a perfect monotone relationship between merit and salary.

The following procedures are suggested for salary equity studies. First, establish a measure of merit. Merit should be based on a composite of such indices as years of experience and publication record. Although merit could be the clinical judgment of a department head or the result of a computation based on a multiple regression equation designed to model existing salaries, merit should be defined by the formula that best reproduces judgments of equitable salaries for hypothetical cases. Second, to detect group bias, study both the difference in merit between the groups holding salary constant and the difference in salary holding merit constant. Third, to remove inequities, one should distribute raises on the basis of both merit and the difference between salary deserved on the basis of merit and actual salary. If applied to all individuals, this method eliminates both individual and group-related inequities in a reasonable time period.

Notes

1. Lord (1967) pointed out a similar paradox, in which analysis of covariance showed that boys' weights exceeded girls' weights even though there was no average weight gain for either group and initial weight was used as a covariate to adjust final weights. In figure 1 of Lord (1967) both correlation ellipses fall on the same principal axis, consistent with equation 10.1. Therefore equation 10.3 shows why analysis of covariance could not remove Lord's group difference.

2. "Good old boy" refers to a person who can succeed on the basis of factors unrelated to merit or quality of performance.

3. The statistical arguments presented here have relevance for other applications of multiple regression. For example, the one-factor hypothesis would be an attractive definition of test fairness because it resolves the apparent contradictions among the four models considered by Darlington (1971), which are unnecessarily restrictive special cases of equation 10.1. Multiple regression has frequently been misused to argue for multiple causation, without testing the one-factor model (Brewer, Campbell, and Crano, 1970). Unless all the variables have been independently experimentally manipulated, it is inappropriate to argue for multiple causes.

References

Adams, J.S. "Inequity in Social Exchange." In *Advances in Experimental Social* mbmbmbmbmbmbmbmbmbmbm

Anderson, N.H. "Equity Judgments as Information Integration." *Journal of Personality and Social Psychology* 33 (1976):291-299.

Bayer, A.E., and Astin, H.S. "Sex Differentials in the Academic Reward System." *Science* 188 (1975):796-802.

Bergmann, B.R., and Maxfield, M. "How to Analyze the Fairness of Faculty Women's Salaries on Your Own Campus." *AAUP Bulletin* 61 (1975):262-265.

Birnbaum, M.H. (a) "The Nonadditivity of Personality Impressions." *Journal of Experimental Psychology* 102 (1974):537-539.

Birnbaum, M.H. (b) "Reply to the Devil's Advocates: Don't Confound Model Testing and Measurement." *Psychological Bulletin* 81 (1974) 854-859.

Braskamp, L.A., Muffo, J.A., and Langston, I.W. "1976 Salary Equity Study University of Illinois at Urbana-Champaign," 1976.

Braskamp, L.A., Muffo, J.A., Langston, I.W. "Determining Salary Equity: Policies, Procedures, and Problems. *Journal of Higher Education* 49 (1978):231-246.

Brewer, M.B., Campbell, D.T., and Crano, W.D. "Testing a Single-Factor Model as an alternative to the Misuse of Partial Correlations in Hypothesis-Testing Research." *Sociometry* 33 (1970):1-11.

Darlington, R.B. "Another Look at 'Cultural Fairness.' " *Journal of Educational Measurement* 8 (1971):71-82.

Dawes, R.M. "Shallow Psychology." In *Cognition and Social Behavior,* ed. J.S. Carroll and J.W. Payne. Hillsdale, N.J.: Erlbaum, 1976.

Ferber, M., and Loeb, J. "Rank, Pay, and Representation of Women on the Faculty at the Urbana-Champaign Campus at the University of Illinois : A Reappraisal," 1977.

Gordon, N.M., Morton, T.E., and Braden, I.C. "Faculty Salaries : Is There Discrimination by Sex, Race, and Discipline?" *American Economic Review* 64 (1974):419-427.

Harris, R.J. "Handling Negative Inputs : On the Plausible Equity Formulae." *Journal of Experimental Social Psychology* 12 (1976):194-209.

Johnson, G.E., and Stafford, F.P. "The Earning and Promotion of Women Faculty." *American Economic Review* 64 (1974):888-903.

Katz, D.A. "The Determinants of Faculty Salaries and Rates of Promotion at a Large University." Doctoral Dissertation, University of Illinois, Urbana-Champaign, 1971.

Katz, D.A. Faculty Salaries, Promotions, and Productivity at a Large University. *American Economic Review* 63 (1973):469-477.

Koch, J.V., and Chizmar, J.F. *The Economics of Affirmative Action.* Lexington, Mass.: Lexington Books, D.C. Heath and Company, 1976.

Lord, F.M. "A Paradox in the Interpretation of Group Comparisons." *Psychological Bulletin* 68 (1967):304-305.

Malkiel, B.G., and Malkiel, J.A. "Male-Female Pay Differentials in Professional Employment." *American Economic Review* 63 (1973):693-705.

Miller, G.A. *Psychology: The Science of Mental Life.* New York: Harper & Row, 1962, pp. 129-146.

Nevill, D.D. "Achieving Salary Equity." *Educational Record* 56 (1975):226-270.

Reagan, B.B., and Maynard, B.J. "Sex Discrimination in Universities: An Approach through Internal Labor Market Analysis." *AAUP Bulletin* 60 (1974):13-21.

Sawyer, J. "Measurement and Prediction, Clinical and Statistical," *Psychological Bulletin* 66 (1966):178-200.

Scott, E.L. *Higher Education Salary Evaluation Kit.* Washington, D.C.: American Association of University Professors, 1977.

Tuckman, B.H., and Tuckman, H.P. "The Structure of Salaries at American Universities." *Journal of Higher Education* 47 (1976):51-64.

Walster, E., Berscheid, E., and Walster, G.W. "New Directions in Equity Research." *Journal of Personality and Social Psychology* 25 (1973):151-176.

11 The Idiosyncratic Determiners of Salary Differences

John V. Long

This chapter describes the author's experience with in-depth interviews of a random sample of faculty chosen on the basis of stratification on their residual size. He discovered patterns in the personal and idiosyncratic history of their salary determination, including factors such as willingness to bargain at initial appointment; service as a department chairman or assistant or associate dean; conversion from calendar to academic year; bad (or good) economic situations at the time of initial appointment; relationship of supply and demand in the discipline; and a host of other usually nonqualifiable determiners of salary. The author suggests that such an in-depth study of a sample of faculty should be conducted in any salary equity study in order to determine an institution's historical and current salary policies that contribute to salary inequities.

As earlier chapters have pointed out, the issue of salary equity has become a major concern in academe in the last few years. Although for several years voices had been raised for redress of purported bias and discrimination in salaries based on sex, race, or ethnic group membership, little was actually done by the colleges and universities to systematically examine or address the issue of salary equity until passage of the Education Amendments of 1972 threatened a possible cutoff of federal dollars to colleges and universities that violated provisions of the law. Given this coercive aspect of the law and the lack of clear procedural guidelines from those who wrote and enforced the law, universities have been groping for a system to bring them in compliance. Most want to satisfy those who have been the alleged subjects of discrimination in salaries while retaining the capability to pay their faculty salaries that are based in some measure on their accomplishments and contributions.

Most examinations of the issues surrounding salary equity appear to be converging on agreement that multiple regression techniques hold the most promise for identifying salary inequity based on sex. Extension of multiple linear regression techniques to issues surrounding inequities based on race, ethnic class membership, and so forth, are unlikely because of the small number of individuals in these categories currently employed at our universities. While I do not oppose the development and application of mathematical models in the identification phase of examining issues surrounding salary equity, I would like to caution those whose enthusiasm for the models might lead to the model *qua* model as the primary or even sole basis for salary adjustments. (See chapter 8.) Most people addressing the equity analysis question do not have tools sophisticated enough to identify and measure the many *qualitative* issues, much less reduce them to a form that can be used as reliable input in developing an adequate mathematical model of a university's salary structure. My primary purpose is to describe a nonstatistical technique that supplements statistical analysis. I will return to the inadequacy of current measures at the end of this chapter.

Using the Interview To Go beyond Regression

During 1976-77 I was part of an internal research team charged with examining the current salary structure at the University of Rhode Island and the concomitant development of a plan to insure that men and women were paid equally for equal work. After reviewing the available literature, we began to consider various ways of fulfilling its charge. Based on the substantial literature supporting the use of multiple regression (Kieft, Astin and Bayer, and so forth), we rejected the more traditional system of examining group averages and making paired comparisons. (See chapter 1 for more description of the paired-comparison technique.) Consequently we used a multiple regression model. But we were concerned about using a statistical procedure that would predict salaries from a finite set of input variables, since most hiring and promotion policies place at least some emphasis on attributes that are hard to quantify.

After completing the initial statistical analyses of the salary data available in personnel files and from other standard sources, we determined that idiosyncratic origins of salary differences could be identified only in face-to-face interviews. Since interviewing the entire faculty was impractical, a random sampling within a stratified distribution of the population was divided according to sex and then stratified according to salary residual (errors of prediction using the regression equation, or more simply the difference between predicted and actual salary). Twenty-four intervals of salary residual were developed. Within each, one male and one female were to be chosen at random. However, because of the low proportion of women in the salary population (189, or 27 percent of the total), several of the twenty-four intervals had no women. Even when intervals were combined to make each one larger and hence increase the likelihood of having a woman in each, we found that some residual intervals still had none or only one woman. Therefore we sampled randomly with the fewer intervals, choosing two men and two women from each interval whenever two or more were available. As a result the final interview sample of forty-three faculty started out with fewer women (18) than men (25). There was some attrition in the interview sample: one woman declined to be interviewed; one male was virtually impossible to reach, did not return phone calls, and did not respond to written communications; three others who were willing to be interviewed declined to complete a supplementary data sheet on scholarly production. We attempted to ascertain whether the scholarly production record of these individuals was in any way exceptional. We determined informally that two of three had a long and scholarly career, while the other, having only recently entered the profession, had virtually no scholarship record. We therefore determined that the absence of scholarship data on these individuals would not seriously affect the analysis.

A comprehensive outline of our procedures can be found in chapter 9. Here I will just describe the outcomes and highlight some of the comments by the interviewees which show the immense difficulty associated with attempts to identify—much less quantify—the myriad factors that individual faculty members perceive as having an impact on their salaries. A complete copy of the interview protocol appears in the appendix.

Scholarship

Faculty at a university are expected to make positive contributions in three traditional areas. These areas—teaching, research, and service—should therefore be considered when examining whether differences between predicted and actual salaries are inequitable or are based on differential contributions. In the brief history of studies examining salary equity, however, only the research and scholarly activity has received much attention (Bayer and Astin, 1975; Darland et al., 1973), with results indicating that scholarly productivity (as measured by number of books, articles, chapters) is among the most important variables in predicting salaries. Our interviews and data sheets regarding scholarly productivity—which were somewhat broader in scope than normal and provided categories for more discipline-specific activities—tended to yield data quite similar to those obtained in earlier studies. Scholarly productivity indices were strongly related to both actual and predicted salary, with correlations of 0.65 and 0.57, respectively. (A complete description of the derivation of this index appears in chapter 9. Scholarship was not included in the regression model because it was not available except on the interview sample.) The typical male faculty member was three times as likely to have published a journal article and twice as likely to have presented a paper at a national conference, and the overall scholarly productivity index for males was 3 1/2 times that for females. These data, within certain philosophical boundaries, might be seen and have been interpreted by some as "justification" for differentials in salary between males and females, but the data still need to be interpreted in light of the emphasis on and opportunity for publication in various disciplines. Abramson (1975) and Centra (1974) note that women are more likely to be found in disciplines and positions where research and publication are more difficult and where the major emphasis is on teaching, while men are more likely to be in positions requiring and conducive to scholarly production.

As we anticipated, the questions asked in the faculty interviews yielded a wealth of information relevant to a study of a university's salary structure. Its implications are significant for a university examining the equity of its salaries and instructive to those contemplating salary equity analyses at their own institutions. Interviews allow the retelling of circumstances as they are recalled by the interviewee. Anyone who spends some time conducting such interviews becomes more aware of the many subtle factors that the interviewees feel have had an impact on their salaries.

Locating the Position

To determine the way in which individuals were first hired and the method used for setting the initial salary, we simply asked the interviewees to tell us in their own words how they first heard of the position. We then followed with a series of probing questions designed to clarify their responses. The responses to these questions were similar for the men and women interviewed. Only about one in five saw an advertisement for the position; one in three made contact at a national conference; one in seven were referred by a major professor. The remainder sent an unsolicited inquiry about positions ("I wanted to relocate in the area. I called one day and asked if there were any openings. They said 'Yes, come on down' and hired me. No formalities. There was a big turnover that year, so there were many opportunities") or had determined that a position was available through some other means ("I felt I was ready for a change; I heard about the opening from a book salesman, applied, and here I am").

Prior Experience

One source of suspected inequity that is often mentioned is based on the assumption that women are more likely than men to be found in disciplines in which they have had extensive previous professional experience that is not taken into account in setting initial salary. In our interview sample we did not find this to be the case. The prior experience of both men and women was very limited; approximately half the sample indicated little or no prior professional experience, and three-quarters reported five years or less for teaching and professional service combined.

Initial Salary

The information we collected indicated that only about one in three new faculty made any effort to negotiate starting salary, although very few recall having seen any published salary for the position. Most expressed regret at not having negotiated harder, now recognizing that little change except lockstep advancement can be accomplished after starting salary is established. As one woman said, "I was hired somewhat higher than most of my colleagues elsewhere and much ahead of [URI colleagues]. I felt very bad about that, but I've become reconciled. . . . I've mellowed" [female interviewee with Ph.D. whose salary placed her above most in her college hired in the preceding few years and most hired thereafter, including new Ph.D's]. The same woman, in illustrating her own campaign to help women entering the professions stated: "Women tend to accept salaries. . . . [They] don't expect to negotiate. . . . I have to teach my students to negotiate." Most faculty interviewed, however, felt there was equity between the salary they received and that given to their colleagues hired at the same time.

Salary Adjustments after Initial Hiring

Although interviewees expressed positive feelings of equity regarding initial salaries, these feelings did not extend to salary increases. Most interviewees expressed feelings of unfair or inequitable treatment. Areas of discontent included new hires, merit, departmental leadership, croneyism, collective bargaining, and departmental philosophy (emphasis on teaching versus research). The following quotes selected from the interviews provide a sense of the areas that the faculty felt led to inequities after their initial employ.

> When I accepted the position, we acknowledged that the salary wasn't very good. They implied that there'd be catch-up, but there hasn't been.

> I think there is a tendency to hire in at higher and higher salaries because we're locked in after that.

> The year after I was hired, the starting salaries for the three new hires were set at five hundred above my and [other new person's] starting salary. . . . We believed that these people were "in step" with us. The chairman even let us help set the starting salaries before we recruited. Then we only got $300 raises ourselves, and the newer people started their first year earning more than us in our second year, even though we helped set what we thought was an equitable starting salary [male].

> A commitment was made that my salary would be "made up" through small annual increments. The commitment was kept only in part. The university and dean began to feel the pinch, and there was little the dean could do.

> I have a problem with those coming in later getting so much more than those who are already here [female interviewee in college with mostly women where starting salaries are getting ahead and leaving the continuing appointments behind—her allegation].

I believe that the starting salaries year after year are going up faster than the wages of the continuing faculty. I also think that those who are hired with special responsibility have it reflected in their starting salaries.

We always felt that the scientists did better than the humanists [member of a humanities department].

One factor in my salary is that I have no Ph.D. in a department where it is the norm. I feel that this may have impacted on the determination of merit and other salary matters.

Before collective bargaining things were pretty hard to pin down. Personalities and so forth had a lot to do with it. Since collective bargaining things have been pretty much OK.

I think that a great deal of it has to do with the power of the chairmen and how hard they fight for their people. I think there are wide differences in starting salaries, especially for the later hirings, and the earlier hirings are not catching up.

The principle around here seems to be that the squeaky wheel gets the grease. Promotions and increases are brought by a fuss.

Merit is not really merit. It's more a personality to personality thing, but not as an attempt to moderate salary inequities.

Historically raises were negotiated. Aggressiveness with the department chairman was required to get a piece of the pie. Merit, of course, was not based on merit. The squeaky wheel and the favorite son surpassed.

Heavy instructional and developmental activities within a small department adversely affected research and publication efforts, which subsequently adversely affected salaries and promotions.

In general I think you'll find that the "inequalities" are largely a function of squeaky wheels and favorite sons. I don't think there have been any systematic biases.

Before collective bargaining it was a one-man show, which resulted in a bimodal distribution with the chairman and his friends at the upper end. There was definitely a cronyism bias. After collective bargaining things are better but often slip through human error. There's still probably some personality getting into it.

As these statements indicate, the feelings of salary inequity by the faculty stem from a wide variety of sources. Even more interesting to the research team, however, was that many of these statements were made by faculty whose actual salaries were substantially more than was predicted by the regression model.

Other Sources of Salary Variation

In addition to responses to direct questions, some other elements of salary history were revealed in the interviews that can account, on an individual basis, for some of the anomalies in salaries. One factor that surfaced repeatedly was compensation for administrative service. There appear to be two types of salary variation related to administrative compensation. Several interviewees received additional compensation for performing administrative roles and managed to keep at least part of the salary supplement when they relinquished the administrative duties. One chairman reported that he was converted from a calendar-year appointment to an academic-year salary with no reduction in salary—the same net effect as a 20 percent raise! He was told by his dean that the conversion was necessary to reduce the total number of faculty on calendar appointments—presumably an economy measure—but the reduction of duties without a commensurate reduction of salary is certainly an interesting economy measure! This same chairman currently receives a chairman's supplement of $1,000 as part of the collective bargaining agreement.

Comments made in the interviews regarding the administrative duty-related salary changes included these illustrative examples.

> I was given an extra thousand for being the director of [research and academic unit], and when I gave the position up, I kept it.

> About ten years ago I switched from calendar to academic contract with no reduction in pay.

> I had the chairmanship of the department, and when I gave it up I had an agreement with the dean that my pay would only be reduced by half of the calendar supplement. That, in part, made up for a number of years of relatively low pay.

Even though, as this last quotation witnesses, some of the decisions regarding keeping supplements may have been designed to adjust for previous inequities, they still have the potential to further imbalance a salary system.

Of greater potential for introducing perceived inequities is the system for assigning salaries to academic deans, heads of research units, and department chairmen who are hired from outside the university primarily to perform in administrative roles. It is widely perceived—and also documented in individual salary comparisons—that these individuals are hired at salaries higher than those paid to people currently employed in comparable positions, and substantially higher than faculty members who have comparable experience. The imbalance in the salary system becomes noticeable when those individuals no longer perform the administrative functions but return to regular faculty status, because the salary differentials are usually part of base salary rather than job-specific supplements that can be withdrawn when the duties are no longer being performed.

Interviewees' Perception of Inequity

Our interviews closed with a general request for comments on any issue regarding salaries or sex-linked bias in salaries at the university. Surprisingly the women tended to express a lesser sense of inequity than the men, and both men and women seemed to sense inequities, if at all, between themselves and their colleagues regardless of gender.

> As far as the difference between men and women is concerned . . . I don't think so. . . . It may have been true in certain areas . . . any of the departments that were women-dominated. My department [humanities] had a healthy mix of men and women and at one time a woman chairman. We had no problems [female].

> I was the first women hired in my rank. I feel that the university has always acted in good faith in dealings with me. I don't think the university has ever been unfair to me. I came here, in part, because I'd been treated unfairly at [another state university], and I left there just as a good affirmative action program got started [female].

> Considerable inequalities in salaries also stem from the fact that faculty hired more recently were started at higher salaries than those who have faithfully served URI for many years. During my time at URI I could not fail to notice that conscientious and good teaching is hardly recognized and is barely rewarded. The faculty's main effort has shifted too far toward research, publication, and attending meetings, and thus the undergraduate student has become the sacrificial lamb on the altar of the almighty dollar—a fact we do not talk about and never put into print [male].

> I think in general that there is a male-female pay differential but that there is also a certain difference set up by the main campus-extension distance and that the teachers of adults are somehow second-class citizens. Some of this is due to the perceptions that Kingston faculty have about us over committee work [female].

Summary and Some Concluding Remarks

As the preceding sections have pointed out, there are a large number of factors that the faculty members interviewed felt had impact on their salaries. Some of these factors would be relatively simple to identify and quantify; others are extremely difficult to identify, much less quantify. Of the three major faculty activities—teaching, research, service—the empirical part of our study looked only at research. Even there our examination, like virtually all others in the literature, was only a quantitative rather than a qualitative look at scholarly production.

In view of the extreme difficulty in identifying and quantifying variables whose impact on salaries is justified (quality of teaching, research, and service), as well as comparable difficulty for variables whose impact is not justified (bias in initial salaries, promotion rates), the development and application of a statistical model that attempts to predict salary from a finite set of quantifiable variables will of necessity be restricted to variables that are relatively easy to define and quantify. While many of these variables may be correlated with salary and hence may explain (even if in mediated form) a portion of the variance in the salaries at a university, the use of models based on these variables appears to be limited to a gross examination of salaries and to the identification of individuals who can then undergo a review process to determine what, if any, adjustments are appropriate. (See chapter 4 for a discussion of specification bias.)

Some have argued that the use of a committee review system for redressing inequities often places the aggrieved individual in the position of being reviewed by those responsible for the inequity. But the complex network of factors that affect university salaries makes this system appear more rational than formulaic adjustment. Identification and redress of previous inequities—like the statistical models themselves—is an iterative process, where the initial iteration is the generation and use of a statistical model and where final iterations necessary for convergence on "equity" are based on the collective judgment of peers.

The much maligned tradition of collegiality and peer review, recent advents in collective bargaining notwithstanding, thus appears to provide the forum for final decisions regarding equity adjustments in salary. If, despite the current awareness regarding issues of sex and other forms of discrimination in salaries, we no longer have confidence in our peers' ability to render unbiased decisions, then our alternative is probably to accept the statistical models as the final arbiter of salaries, and we should move toward development and adoption of similar models for decisions such as promotion, tenure, and merit. Perhaps at some time in the distant future our systems for identification and measurement of the network of attributes that constitutes a faculty member will be developed so that this becomes possible. For tomorrow and through perhaps 2006 (my projected retirement date), however, I doubt that we will reach that point.

References

Abramson, Joan. *The Invisible Woman.* Washington, D.C.: Jossey-Bass, 1975.
Bayer, Alan E., and Astin, Helen S. "Sex Differentials in the Academic Reward System." *Science* 188 (May 23, 1975):796-802.

Carnegie Commission on Higher Education, *Opportunities for Women in Higher Education: Their Current Participation, Prospects for the Future, and Recommendations for Action.* New York: McGraw-Hill, 1973.

Centra, John A., *Women, Men, and the Doctorate.* Princeton, N.J.: Educational Testing Service, 1974.

Darland, M.G., Dawkins, S.M., Lavasich, J.L., Scott, E.L., Sherman, M.E., and Whipple, J.L., "Application of Multivariate Regression to Studies of Salary Differences between Men and Women Faculty." *Proceedings of the Social Statistics Section*, Washington, D.C., American Statistical Association, 1973, pp. 120-132.

Kieft, Raymond N., "Are Your Salaries Equal?" *College Management* 9 no. 23 (April 1974):23.

Appendix:
Suggested Salary
Inequity Interview
Protocol

NAME _____

FACULTY SALARY INTERVIEW

1. Please verify that the following information is accurate regarding your faculty history

INFORMATION	CHECK HERE IF ACCURATE	PUT REVISIONS HERE IF INACCURATE
A. Year of first appointment	_____	_____
B. Starting rank	_____	_____
C. Starting salary	_____	_____
D. Age at first appointment	_____	_____
E. Doctorate awarded in	_____	_____
F. Years of professional work prior to current position	_____	_____
G. Date tenure was effective	_____	_____
H. Date of promotion to assistant professor	_____	_____
I. Date of promotion to associate professor	_____	_____
J. Date of promotion to full professor	_____	_____
K. Salary for 1975-1976 year	_____	_____

1a. Please enter the number of each of the following types of scholarly work in the spaces below.

	Prior to current Appointment		Since current Appointment	
	Sole Author	Team Author	Sole Author	Team Author
Book (original)				
Monograph				
Chapter in a book				
Article in a refereed journal				
Article in a non-refereed journal				
Newsletter article				
Editor of a book of readings				
Author of a proposed grant				
Author of a funded grant				
Paper presented at a regional conference				
Paper presented at a national conference				
Short story or poem published				
Presenter in a one-person show				
Other				
Other				
Other				

2. How did you come to be employed at (institution)? (Allow the
    interviewee to describe in his/her own words the conditions under
    which he/she was first employed: e.g., "How did you hear of the
    opening?... Did you hear of (institution) prior to knowledge of
    the opening?... Were you solicited?... Referred by major
    professor?... (Probe for other evidences of the "old boy"
    network).

    _____

    _____

    _____

    _____

    _____

    _____

    _____

    _____

    _____

    _____

    _____

    _____

    _____

3. How many years did you have in a university or college in a faculty
    position (exclude teaching assistant or grad assistant positions)
    prior to your first employ at (institution)?

4. How many years did you have in your professional field when first
    employed at (institution), excluding university or college faculty
    positions?

5. Did your first appoingment at (institution) include a special
    function such as chairman_____ director_____ associate director____

                        dean_____ associate dean_____ assistant dean_____

                        grant director_____ coordinator_____

                        other?

    SPECIFICALLY:_____

    _____

6. When you were first hired, was your appointment unusual in any way?

    For example: temporary_____ grant funds_____

                        sabbatical replacement_____ higher/lower-rank
                                                       than usual_____

                        other_____ SPECIFICALLY_____

                        _____

                        _____

7. If the answer to number 5 or 6 was yes, was there any renogotiation
    when you relinquished the special duties or changed status?

    No_____   Yes_____ SPECIFICALLY_____

    _____

    _____

8. Do you currently have a special role or title? _____

    During your career at (institution), have you ever had a special role,
    function or title?_____

9. If the answer to number 8 was yes, was any special stipend or salary
    adjustment made with the position?_____

    If so, was it (will it be) relinquished with the responsibility?

    _____

10. In the year in which you were hired, were people in your field finding it easy to secure positions?_____

11. Did you have several competing offers when you were first hired at (institution)?   _____

12. Did you get the starting salary you wanted?

    _____

13. Did you counter the institution's first offer with a demand of your own?   _____

    How many offers and counter-demands were made in all?

    _____

14. Was a salary or range of salaries advertised with the vacancy notice or other first notification of the position?

    _____

    If so, was the starting salary you received outside of the range advertised?_____ Above? _____

    Above, by how much?   _____

15. When you were hired, did you get the impression, or did you in fact <u>know</u>, that you were selected by the institution <u>a priori</u> (through reputation, publications, friendships, recommendations by your major professor, ...) and then the rank and salary were set with you in mind?   _____

    (Rephrase if unclear)

    Describe the circumstances_____

    _____

    _____

    _____

    _____

    _____

16. When you were hired, did you feel that you were hired <u>in</u> <u>step</u>
     with the rest of you colleagues at other institutions?

                         If <u>no</u>, how so?   _____

     When you were hired did you feel that you were hired <u>in</u> <u>step</u>
     with those hired in the preceding couple of years in your
     department?
                         If <u>no</u>, how so?   _____

     Have those hired in your department since your first employ
     been hired <u>in</u> <u>step</u> with the salary paid at your first employ?

                         If <u>no</u>, how so?   _____

17. Were you hired with the terminal degree in hand. ("Terminal
     degree" means highest degree appropriate to your field, not
     highest degree you hold.) If <u>yes</u>, go to <u>18</u>.
                                                      _____

     Were you hired with the understanding that you would complete
     the terminal degree shortly?
                                                      _____

     were you hired with the understanding that there would be an
       ajustment in salary or rank upon completion of that degree?

           If <u>yes</u>, describe _____

     _____

     _____

     Was such an adjustment made when you did in fact complete
     that degree?
                                                      _____

18. During the years since your initial employ at (institution) there
     have been a number of adjustments in salary for people hired during
     adverse economic circumstances, or in over-supplied disciplines or
     in <u>over</u> the salaries of those already on the staff, despite similar
     qualifications. Have any such adjustments been made for you?
                                                      _____

     SPECIFICALLY_____

     _____

     _____

Have you ever made a formal or informal request for such
a salary review and adjustment?
_____

If <u>yes</u>, what was the outcome?_____

_____

_____

19. At your first hiring at (institution) were any commitments for a
     subsequent adjustment in salary or rank other than for the
     completion of a terminal degree?
     _____

     If <u>yes</u>, describe_____

     _____

     If <u>yes</u>, was this commitment kept?_____

     _____

20. During your years at URI were you ever given any non-routine
     increases (or decreases) in salary?
     _____

     If <u>yes</u>, what were the circumstances of those?_____

     _____ _____

     _____

21. Were there any other peculiar circumstances surrounding your
     first employment at URI, or are there other facts concerning
     your current salary at URI that are worth noting in this survey?

About the Contributors

Roy M. Ageloff received the Ph.D. from the University of Massachusetts. He is an associate professor of management science at the University of Rhode Island. His primary research interest is the application of management information systems and simulation models to college and university planning.

Michael H. Birnbaum received the doctorate from the University of California at Los Angeles and is now an associate professor of psychology at the University of Illinois at Urbana-Champaign. His research involves development and testing of mathematical theories of human judgment. He has investigated topics ranging from theoretical issues in psychophysics to social judgments, including moral evaluation, personality impression formation, and integration of information provided by sources who vary in expertise and bias. His interest in merit and equity evaluation stems from a desire to see that principles and techniques developed in the laboratory are applied to problems of practical judgment.

Larry Braskamp has been a faculty member at the University of Nebraska, Lincoln, in the Department of Educational Psychology. From 1974 to 1976 he was assistant to the chancellor at the university. In 1976 he came to the University of Illinois as head of the Measurement Research Division of the Office of Instructional Resources. His research interests are evaluation in higher education and utilization of evaluative information.

Larry O. Hunter received the M.Ed. from Harvard University. He has served as a secondary school teacher and public school administrator and is presently the director of management information services at the University of Idaho. He is active in the Association for Institutional Research, and his current research interests are higher-education policy analysis and cost analysis.

Ira W. Langston IV has been the coordinator of research and testing in the University Office of School and College Relations at the University of Illinois since 1972. He is responsible for conducting research relating to admissions and financial aid. In addition, he worked for four years with the Council on Program Evaluation on the Urbana campus of the university. His recent interests include studies of programs for disadvantaged students and trend analysis for institutional planning. He received his training at the University of Illinois.

John V. Long received the Ph.D. from Syracuse University. He has served as a teacher of high school mathematics and is currently an associate professor of education at the University of Rhode Island, where most of his responsibilities are as a senior research scientist in the Curriculum Research and Development

Center. His primary research interests are in applied measurement and educational research, particularly as they apply to issues in the education of disadvantaged students.

Mary P. Martin is a Ph.D. candidate in institutional research at Florida State University. She spent the fall of 1978 with the Organization of Economic Cooperation and Development (OECD) in Paris and with the University of Technology, Department of Management Studies, Loughborough, England, as part of her program of studies as an intern. Before entering graduate school, Ms. Martin was the director of institutional research at the University of North Dakota.

P. Kenneth Morse received the Ph.D. in education and psychology from the University of Michigan. Currently serving as professor of dental education and coordinator of management planning at the Medical College of Georgia, he previously served as director of evaluation services at Eastern Michigan University and supervisor of program planning for the Michigan Bureau of Higher Education. He has specialized in institutional research, with an interest in projections and simulations.

John A. Muffo is assistant director of the Office of Administrative Studies at the University of Illinois at Urbana-Champaign. He has also worked in the institutional research offices at the University of Denver and Metropolitan State College. His primary research interest is the improvement of management information for decision making in higher education.

Glenworth A. Ramsay is an associate professor of economics at the University of Rhode Island, where he teaches graduate econometrics. He received the Ph.D. from Boston College. Although his principal research interest is industrial organization, he has recently become interested in applying mathematical and statistical techniques to institutional problems.

Barbara Hauben Tuckman is currently director of the center for Economic Education at Florida State University and also serves as assistant to the university president. She received the M.A. and the Ph.D. in economics from the University of Wisconsin and Florida State University, respectively. In addition to teaching economics, she has worked in the Department of Revenue for the State of Wisconsin and for the Federal Trade Commission in Washington. Her research interests include economics of education, industrial organization, and economic education and development.

Robert E. Wall is a graduate professor of education at Towson State University. He has served as director of research and evaluation and has taught in the psychology, computer science, and health science departments. He received the Ph.D. at the University of Maryland. His principal professional interests are statistics, research, and evaluation.

John D. Williams is the chairperson and a professor in educational measurement and statistics at the University of North Dakota. His research has included developing models in multiple linear regression. He has investigated the relationships of several variables to faculty salaries.

About the Editors

Thomas R. Pezzullo received the Ph.D. from Boston College. He has served as a teacher of mathematics and science in the Newton, Massachusetts, public schools and is an associate professor of education at the University of Rhode Island, where he also serves as assistant vice-president for academic affairs. He has held the position of director of the Curriculum Research and Development Center and is the co-author of *Education, Inequality, and National Policy* (Lexington Books, 1976). His principal research interest is educational policy, particularly as it relates to the disadvantaged, compensatory programs, and the genetic-environmental controversy.

Barbara E. Brittingham received the Ph.D. in educational research from Iowa State University. She is currently acting dean of the College of Human Science and Services at the University of Rhode Island and associate professor of education. Her research interests are salary equity analyses, program evaluation, and educational innovation. She has served as affirmative action officer of the university and director of the university's Curriculum Research and Development Center.